The Family Devotions IdeaBook

The Family Devotions Idea Book

Evelyn Blitchington

BETHANY HOUSE PUBLISHERS
MINNEAPOLIS, MINNESOTA 55438
A Division of Bethany Fellowship, Inc.

Copyright © 1982
Evelyn Blitchington
All rights reserved

Published by Bethany House Publishers
A Division of Bethany Fellowship Inc.
6820 Auto Club Road, Minneapolis, Minnesota 55438

Printed in the United States of America

Library of Congress Cataloging in Publication Data

Blitchington, Evelyn, 1947-
   The family devotions idea book.

   Bibliography: p.
   1. Family—Prayer-books and devotions—
English.   I. Title.
BV255.B47   249   82-4252
ISBN 0-87123-254-5   AACR2

The Author

EVELYN BLITCHINGTON is married and the mother of two children. She graduated with honors from Mary Washington College in 1969. She has worked as a personnel assistant, a dental receptionist and office manager, and as a social worker for Aid to Dependent children. She is very active in her church, teaching both kindergarten and adolescent age groups. She wrote *Adolescent Growth and Development* for the Home Study Institute in 1976 and is a member of Psi Chi, an honorary fraternity in psychology.

Foreword

Here is some good news! No one will have as much influence on your child as you do—if you want that influence and are willing to start early. Many parents are eager to take the time and seize that opportunity.

A happy child is a child that has a value system. That's where loving parents make the difference. They are around when the child needs them and they are teaching the important concepts of life. Part of teaching that value system is introducing the child to Jesus Christ.

This book contains a ton of ideas to help a concerned parent introduce his child to Christ. Shop through these pages. Pick out the suggestions that fit your mix. Many of the plans are fantastic!

By furnishing guidelines for your child, by becoming involved in his life, you will know the satisfaction of helping him grow into a balanced adult.

William L. Coleman

Introduction

Reason tells you nothing should grow there. Yet, hundreds of feet below ground, in the cool darkness of the coal mine, the pure white apple moss thrives. In spite of the black dust that coats the ceilings, floors, and walls of the mine, the plant's leaves remain unsmudged—a natural wax coating causes every speck of dust to slide off, leaving not a trace of black. The apple moss stands in sharp contrast to its gritty surroundings, a symbol of purity amidst the blackness of the mine.

This is what we want for ourselves and our families—to flourish, pure and unblemished, in a world polluted by sin's sordid darkness. But how do *we* get the protective "wax" that shields us from sin?

The Psalmist gives the answer: "Thy word have I hid in mine heart, that I might not sin against thee" (Ps. 119:11). As individuals and families, we are to "come boldly before the throne of grace." Face-to-face with God, we are to learn from His Word and receive His guidance, blessing, and victory over evil. We must, therefore, establish a family altar, a time and place where family members can meet God together.

This family altar can take many forms, depending upon individual needs within the family. In this book you will find many suggestions for family worship. You probably won't use all of them, but on these pages you will find ideas to make your family's worship time interesting, meaningful, and spiritually productive.

If you do not conduct family worship in your home, there is no better time to begin than *today.*

Contents

PART ONE

A Necessity, Not a Luxury

1. Why Have Family Worship?

Two brothers solemnly entered the doorway of the musty, run-down farmhouse which had belonged to their parents. The older was to marry soon. Since both brothers were carpenters, they planned to tear down the old home and build a new one in which the newlyweds would begin their life together.

As the men walked slowly from room to room, they reminisced about the happy years they had spent there as children. They compared memories of playing baseball in the front yard and camping under the willow tree in the backyard. They recalled the hours spent polishing the maple floors and painting the wide front porch. Nostalgic sorrow clouded their minds as they thought of tearing down this home where they were born and grew to manhood.

They entered the kitchen and gazed at the table standing in the center of the cracked linoleum floor—yes, it was the very one they and their parents had used. The two stood in silence, recalling the many times their family had gathered there to eat and to fellowship. The men could almost see the large black family Bible that their father had read from each morning. They could almost hear him praying, holding each member of the family up before God as the day began.

They knowingly glanced at each other in embarrassment. Though they admired and emulated their father, they both had failed to cultivate his intimate walk with God.

The older brother's words broke the silence. "You know, I

have so much more than Mom and Dad ever dreamed of having. But I've felt that somehow their life was better than mine is; something is missing. And now I realize what it is. When I begin my new life with Nancy, I'm going to follow in Mom and Dad's footsteps; I'm going to start each day with God."

"Why wait till then?" his brother replied. "Let's both start tomorrow."

In all likelihood you believe, as did these brothers, that family worship is an important, if not imperative, aspect of the Christian life. And whether they call it family devotions, family worship, family altar, or whatever, the vast majority of Christians would agree that it is important even though many of them do not maintain a family altar. In fact, one recent study showed that while nearly all members of a certain Christian denomination believed in the value of family worship, and at one time or another had tried to have regular devotions at home, only sixty percent of them were regularly conducting home worship.

It takes time, effort, and persistence to have *daily* family worship. But the rewards are great, benefiting the family both now and for eternity.

Let's examine each reward in turn:

1. *Home worship helps each family member know Christ better.* The purpose of home worship is not to entertain, although this may be a by-product of some worship sessions. If we emphasize worship as fun rather than sacred we will miss its true significance. Besides, how can we compete with the world's fun (television, movies, amusement parks) in this day when so much emphasis is placed on entertainment and pleasure-seeking?

Prepare children to accept Christ.

A primary concern in home worship is studying and discovering God's vital interest in each family member and the way each can have a personal relationship with the Creator and Ruler of the universe. *We are to prepare our children to accept Christ as their personal Lord and Savior.*

Author Barbara Cook was skeptical when her four-year-old approached her, begging, "Mommy, pray with me. I want to take Jesus as my Savior." Now she insists, ". . . you may never know until your child is grown about the relationship he's developing with God right now. His young lips can't always verbalize it, but if you've brought him to Jesus, first as a baby, then as a toddler, as a kindergartner and a first grader, you can be sure Jesus is responding to him as he's responding to Jesus.*

Once a person accepts Christ, his daily communion with Christ enables the person to know Him better, to discern His will, to understand and appreciate the sacrifice He made on our behalf. An Acquaintance becomes a cherished Friend as time is spent with Him, discussing personal hopes and disappointments, and sharing all of life's events, both great and small.

2. *Home worship provides each family member with spiritual nourishment.* Even recently, some well-meaning religious leaders neglected content teaching—the "strong meat" of the Gospel— in favor of what they considered improved teaching methods. They stressed love and warmth, happiness and fun, with little emphasis on doctrine, principles, and the laws of God. They thought that, given the most positive environment possible, children would develop lovely characters.

Unfortunately these religious leaders discovered too late that no one "drifts" into character. The youths reared without clear biblical doctrine and principles had no absolutes upon which to base their actions; they were unable to make choices between right and wrong when they were old enough to think for themselves. This is no doubt one of the reasons for the epidemic of divorce among Christians. These people have grown up learning to follow their feelings, rather than God's mandate for faithfulness to one's mate.

Teach biblical values and principles. During family worship, we are to teach our children (and learn ourselves) to live "soberly, righteously, and godly, in this present world" (Titus 2:12). We are to pass on to them the values and principles as well as the vast historical and literary resources of the Bible. We are to acquaint them with great biblical truths which can guide them from childhood through old age. We are to challenge them to accept Christ's call to self-sacrfice, humility, and service. We are to

How to Raise Good Kids by Barbara Cook (Bethany House Publishers, 1978), p. 83.

teach them that all the world offers is truly shallow in comparison with the riches of Christ.

Teach children to apply truth.

3. *Home worship teaches children to internalize values.* 2 Timothy 2:15 tells us, "Study to shew thyself approved unto God, a workman that needeth not to be ashamed, rightly dividing the word of truth." Family worship provides a time to help each family member *apply* the truths of Scripture in day-to-day situations of life.

Pray about specific family problems.

A young mother experienced great shock and heartache as her six-year-old daughter's kindergarten teacher confided, "Lisa has some problems in social relations. She's very bossy around the other children and is sometimes cruel to them."

This mother and her husband discussed the problem with each other and with the girl. But it seemed no real progress was made until finally the family began having worship together, reading from the Scriptures and praying.

Two weeks after the family began this experiment in faith, the mother joyfully reported, "Lisa has already begun to overcome her problems at school. And we owe it all to the power of prayer!"

This mother had prayed about the specific problem in front of the entire family and had claimed the Lord's promises to help those who trust in Him. Soon she was reaping the rewards of faith. She regrets only that she let so many years go by without daily family worship.

The responsibility for applying biblical truths rests with the parents, but sometimes younger family members will show unexpected insight. One family read the Twenty-third Psalm aloud every day for a week during family worship. Their three-and-a-half-year-old daughter sat quietly during each recitation. But to everyone's amazement, she had memorized the Psalm by the end of the week! Her family was pleased but assumed that she was too young to understand what she was saying. They soon learned differently.

The girl and her mother were Christmas shopping, and the

moment the child entered the toy department she began begging for everything in sight. "I want this dolly . . . I want this puzzle . . . I want a bicycle. . . ." On and on she went.

Suddenly she stopped, looked straight at her mother, and said, "I want and want and want—but I mustn't want. Because the Lord is my Shepherd."

Kneel in silence—let God speak to you. Anna Mow has suggested a method by which children can learn to apply God's Word to their own lives (this also gives parents insight on the extent of their children's moral development). She suggests that if a parent discovers his child committing some offense, he should kneel with the child before God *in silence* and wait for God to speak to the child.

One father was particularly skeptical about how well this would work for his four-year-old daughter, but decided to try it anyway. She had written all over the inside cover of an expensive book he had recently purchased. She knew she had done wrong and was awaiting her punishment.

Instead of spanking her, he asked her to kneel with him for prayer. She kneeled and immediately began praying out loud.

He interrupted her, saying, "This time we will be quiet and let God talk to us."

After a few moments he asked, "Has God told you anything?"

"Yes," she answered. "God told me that I should never write in your books again and that I should erase what I wrote today."

Interest your child in Bible heroes. 4. *Home worship helps family members learn more about the Bible.* Most pre-schoolers today know the names of every muppet on "The Muppet Show," but don't know the names of Adam and Eve's sons. Our teenagers can sing scores of rock songs by heart but have not memorized a single passage of Scripture. What a sad commentary on our Christian commitment!

Home worship can help remedy this situation if we emphasize learning and understanding the Bible. Toddlers can grow up admiring David instead of Batman; teenagers can emulate Christ rather than rock star, Mick Jagger. A noted student of the Bible declares that the Bible will challenge young people's imaginations and abilities to the very limit—as long as their minds haven't been warped by worldly overstimulation.

6. *Home worship provides for individual needs.* One powerful reason to establish a family altar is your intimate knowledge of each member of your household. You know what makes each one 'tick"—his likes and dislikes, his temperament, his strengths and weaknesses. Thus you are far better qualified to present to him God's Word—tailored to his individual needs—than is a Sunday school teacher who sees him only one or two hours each week.

Individualize your teaching to meet the most urgent needs. Stress God's many promises of protection to a fearful child. Emphasize God's desire for sacrificial love and service to a strong-willed child.

7. *Home worship promotes family communication.* As parents and children together pray and study God's Word, they realize that they stand before God on common ground. Parents come to realize that their children are precious to the Lord, bought and paid for by Christ's blood. Children begin to understand that their parents, although they are to be obeyed and respected, have trials and temptations just as children do. Consequently, new understanding and appreciation of each other are developed, and lines of communication are opened.

Encourage honesty about personal weaknesses. This requires parents to be honest about their own weaknesses and failures. Accept James's challenge to "confess your faults one to another" (James 5:16). Such candidness can be painful, but its result will be richer relationships.

Consider, for example, the study of obedience. Children can learn in family worship that they are not the only ones who must obey authority. They learn that even Mother and Dad must submit to Christ's authority in every aspect of their lives. Governmental authorities and employers also expect obedience. If the parents speak honestly, the children will also discover that adults have many of the same difficulties with obedience that children do.

When the family prays together about such problems, each member draws strength from the prayerful concern of the others. Mom, Dad, Brother and Sister can each therefore face the day, knowing that their family and their God stand behind them.

However, family worship should not be used as a time for thinly-disguised scolding, as a chance to point out the faults of others. "Let's pray that no one in the family yields to temptation today" is a lot different than "Johnny told a lie today. He's been very naughty lately, so let's pray for him."

Divide into two-person "prayer pairs." If situations arise that are too sensitive to be discussed before the whole family—if, for example, Sister's boyfriend has just broken up with her and she is too heartbroken to pray in front of everyone about it—parents and children can break up into two-person units for prayer (if there is an even number of people). Mother and Sister could pray together about the boyfriend while Brother and Dad pray for Dad's boss who is becoming receptive to the gospel.

In a day when families are so fragmented, we need this kind of close, personal concern for each other. Parents and children both need someone with whom to share their joys and sorrows, someone who loves them enough to open up and show genuine interest in all aspects of their lives.

8. *Home worship helps develop a quiet spirit and sense of tranquillity.* When worshipping with our children, we not only teach them Bible truths and a love for God, we also give them a chance to develop and appreciate "a quiet spirit." Andrew Murray has pointed out that "inward tranquillity is produced by outward tranquillity. . . . The more tranquillity a child has enjoyed in infancy, the more he will possess hereafter."*

Our society emphasizes stimulation. One of the most popular children's television programs offers such a constant barrage of stimulation that adults have been known to get headaches from watching it. Our senses are besieged by noise from automobiles and airplanes, sensual pictures on billboards, and the constant

---

How to Raise Your Children for Christ by Andrew Murray (Bethany House Publishers, 1975), p. 13.

whirl of activity in this fast-moving age. *Amidst this pandemo-
nium, what better gift could we give ourselves and our children
than a period of quietness before God to listen to His gentle
voice?*

One family has chosen to spend a few quiet moments together
before each meal. Their period of silence is broken, not by words,
but by a song of thanksgiving to God. This practice makes it eas-
ier for each family member to experience a continual attitude of
worship.

9. *Home worship testifies to others of your love for Christ.*
Christian parents have two realms of responsibility. First, they
are responsible for each member's spiritual, physical, emotional,
and intellectual well-being. The parents must support each other
and together rear their children for Christ. This is the *internal*
realm of responsibility.

Second, they are responsible to be Christ's ambassadors in a
sin-sick world. This is the *external* realm of responsibility. Christian families are to display before others the love, joy, and peace
that come only from Christ. "By this shall all men know that ye
are my disciples, if you have love one to another" (John 13:35).
When others see the love, firmness, and patience with which the
Christian mother deals with her child, they will want to know her
secret. When little ones break forth in songs of praise to Jesus,
hardened hearts frequently will soften.

Successful witnessing depends upon our continual union with
Christ, "for without me ye can do nothing" (John 15:5). Abraham is a wonderful example of a man who trusted in God and
depended upon God.

> By faith Abraham, when he was called to go out into a
> place which he should after receive for an inheritance,
> obeyed; and he went out, not knowing whither he went. By
> faith he sojourned in the land of promise, as in a strange
> country. . . . (Heb. 11:8, 9)

As Abraham traveled in the land of promise, he built an altar
to God wherever he pitched his tent; on this altar he offered
morning and evening sacrifices. And when he moved on, he left
the altar as a reminder of his devotion to God. Travelers, as they
passed by Abraham's former campground, would see his altar

and know that Abraham had lived there. Our family worship habits may remind others, as Abraham's altars did, that man is to worship the Lord.

Allow "outsiders" to worship with you. Recently my family and I visited a relative in a distant city. During our stay we attempted to have worship time with our young daughter as usual. We would go to a quiet bedroom where we would have worship, supposedly unobserved. But our relative became so intrigued with what we were doing that she asked to join us. Soon she was telling other family members and friends about our worship and was even inviting them to join us. She still talks about how much she enjoyed those times, even months later, all because we faithfully observed our family worship time.

2. Setting the Stage

Establish a "covenant place" for worship.

Where should you have family worship?

No matter what place you choose, *find one special place and stick with it.* You can call this your "covenant place." Whenever you pass this place, or even think about it, your mind will automatically turn to God just as you automatically think of food when you see the dining room table. When you or your child fondly recall meaningful times of worship, you will be able to picture in vivid detail your covenant place; you won't have to scan your home mentally in an attempt to recall where the special meetings with God took place.

Of course, it doesn't really matter where you choose to have worship. Many families like to have a relaxed, informal time around the dining table after a meal. Others choose to gather on a comfortable sofa that is conducive to reading and to kneeling for prayer. One mother of four boys liked to get all her sons ready for bed, then bundle up with them in a big bed for a Bible story, songs, and short prayer.

Worship at the beginning and end of the day.

When should you have family worship?

One of the most important decisions you will need to make is when to have your family worship. Some families have such flexible schedules that they can choose from a wide variety of times, but most people find that they must choose morning or evening, periods when the family is most likely to be together. Let's consider some of the advantages of each.

Worship in the morning sets the tone for the whole day, before responsibilities, worries, and a hundred small details of life have a chance to crowd out thoughts of Jesus. Use this time to thank God for His protection during the night and to ask for help, guidance, and watchcare during the day.

Pray together for the day's agenda. Be specific. You might pray, "Dear Father, please help Paige to not be nervous while she tries out for the gymnastic team today. And please help Mom get all of her cleaning and cooking done before our guests arrive." This will prove much more meaningful to your family than several smooth-sounding generalities. Assure your children that heavenly guardians will accompany them throughout the day, not to spy on them but to give them help, strength, and protection.

Dedicate yourselves to God for that day. A person's mind generally is most fresh and alert in the morning (unless, of course, you are a family of "night people" who don't really gain consciousness until after 10 a.m.) and can thus most easily grasp eternal truths. This is therefore an excellent time for Bible study. If one's first thoughts are of Jesus, his mind can return again and again during the day to what he read or discussed that morning. Biblical principles can then be integrated into one's daily living.

Prayer in the morning can center upon asking God's blessing and guidance upon the family for the entire day. Use this time to dedicate yourselves to God and His service for that day. Great spiritual benefit can be gained if your family has the time and inclination to have early-morning worship.

Many families, on the other hand, find that the morning hours are too hectic for the type of relaxed, unhurried worship they enjoy. They prefer to gather before God at the close of the day, when things are much less rushed.

There are advantages to evening worship besides the more relaxed atmosphere. Evening worship can serve as the climax of every family member's day; it can be the culmination of the day's activities, an event toward which all other activities have been leading. All day long family members encounter trials, temptations, and victories; in their experiences they learn spiritual truths. Therefore, evening worship can center on the day's experiences, the sorrows and joys, the ups and downs. The family members can discuss problems or ideas in the context of the biblical lesson being studied. They can draw closer together as they share their lives with one another under the umbrella of God's love and protection.

Apply Scripture to the day's experiences. If worship centers around studying certain books or chapters in the Bible, then throughout the day family members can be alert for illustrations and anecdotes to shed light on the Scripture portion being studied. This exercise will help keep people's minds on Jesus during the day.

Finally, evening worship can impart a sense of peace and rest at the close of the day. Rather than scurrying around doing a multitude of last-minute chores, rather than sitting transfixed before a television set, the family members can, in an unhurried and reverent spirit, join to praise God for His goodness throughout the day. They can find the joy and peace that God gives and then go to bed uplifted. Can there be a better way to end the day?

Even greater spiritual strength can be obtained by worshiping morning *and* evening—or even worshiping three times a day. The Psalmist wrote, "Evening and morning, and at noon, will I pray" (Ps. 55:17). Surely such a close walk with God, such a regular bowing before His throne is the desire of every Christian. It can give us a special closeness to the Lord, a sense of His participation in every aspect of our lives.

Discuss answers to the morning's prayers. If we present our problems to the Lord in the morning, often in the evening we can have a delightful praise session as we consider the wonderful way He has responded to our pleas. One family I knew faced what seemed an impossible situation. The husband had been unemployed for several months. The family's savings were depleted and the house payment was due the next day.

At morning worship they prayed for guidance, and the Lord directed them to hold a yard sale. As soon as they rose from their knees, they set to work collecting all the furniture, toys, and valuables they didn't need. They set the items out in the yard, erected a sign, and waited on the Lord for the results.

As the day progressed, the money began to trickle in, then pour in. At evening worship they counted their money and sang songs of praise to God as they discovered they had more than enough for their house payment and the next month's grocery expenses.

This was not the end of their problems, however. Several months later they had to repeat the yard sale for another house payment. Eventually they had to sell their house and rent a smaller one, but they continued to trust in God and to praise Him for His care. They had learned, in family worship, the art of "casting all your care upon him; for he careth for you" (1 Pet. 5:7).

Of course, the most important thing is to establish a time when you will best be able to have worship *regularly*. The idea of evening worship might sound great to you, but if your family usually scatters in different directions each evening, choose another time. You may have to make some adjustments in your schedule to accommodate family worship, but you should begin by choosing a time that is most conducive to regularity, preparedness, and fellowship.

Family worship should be the highlight of the day, but it can't be so if we must "hurry so you won't miss the schoolbus," or if the family yawns in unison because it is too late in the day. You must choose what is best for your own family's life-style.

Worship at the *best* time for *your* family. Regular worship carries great benefits. For example, Corrie ten Boom, in *The Hiding Place*, relates that she and her family had morning and evening worship for as long as she could remember. Each morning her father gathered his family and employees around the kitchen table for Bible reading and prayer. Then in the evening he repeated this procedure with the family and any guests that might be in the home.

Corrie describes how she often secretly wished for a short Bible chapter and prayer—evidently every period of worship did not inspire her to do great things for God. But this habitual worship produced a family who loved and served God at any cost. In fact, Corrie's sister, Betsie, before her death in a concentration camp, told Corrie to set up a rehabilitation program for the Nazis, her captors. She loved them despite the cruelty and abuse she suffered at their hands; she longed to help them in any way she could. The worship habit was a keystone in Corrie and Betsie's love for their enemies.

Anna Mow includes in her book a letter from a man who gave up an athletic career to become a minister. His reasons for doing so are very enlightening:

> I have always depended upon God for strength and security and have always tried to do His will. I will attribute the attitudes I have to my home environment. My father is the greatest person in the world. I know no other person who is so versatile, so authoritative, so secure, so sensible, so much at home with himself as my father. I would say that my mother has been the real spiritual backbone of our family. My sister and I were born in the depression. My father was principal of a high school at the depression salary of $640.00 a year. At the same time he was working on his master's degree. . . . From the time I was a first grader Dad farmed one hundred and thirty acres, he and mother both taught school, sometimes twenty miles away, and they were part-time pastors of a church forty miles away.
>
> With planting, plowing, harvesting, paper grading, class parties, funerals, revivals, weddings and preaching, we had a merry time. Mother always had time to check our ears for cleanliness. She always seemed to give us each special attention. Dad always found time to shoot baskets with my brother and me in the barn at chore time. *Most of all, they found time for family worship.** I've seen my father keep men waiting in order to take time for worship with the family. They were always invited in to worship and to eat with us if they would come. Mother wanted everyone to stay to eat, and Dad would call on the guest to give thanks. I am ashamed to say that I laughed to myself more than once at a

*Italics added for emphasis.

plumber or a salesman as he stuttered a prayer. I want to say
that a fellow never forgets such things.*

**If you
can't be a
regular, at
least be
irregular!**

What if you can't have family worship every
day? Maybe Mom teaches two days a week,
Brother has basketball practice each evening,
and Dad works at a part-time job in addition to
his regular one. Of course, daily family worship
is the goal for which we strive, but by all means
don't let your inability to gather daily for worship hinder you from having worship at all.

Perhaps you can gather for worship twice a week, or on week-
ends, or one week out of the month. Whatever your family schedule permits, try to be as regular as possible in keeping this special
appointment with God. Give it top priority in your family's
activities. *Make your other plans fit around family worship*
rather than trying to "squeeze in" a time of worship between Sister's piano lessons and Mom's housecleaning.

How long should worship be?

**Keep it
short.**

Length of your worship time will depend to a
great extent on the ages of the children in your
family. Very small children cannot be expected
to sit reverently for long periods of time and still find the experience enjoyable. You may, of course, be able to force them to "sit
still and be quiet" for lengthy worship sessions. But, if they do so
only out of fear of punishment, or even sheer willpower, then you
have defeated one of the primary purposes of family worship—to
help children love God and desire to serve Him.

Even if your family has older children, you will not want to
make worship so long that it becomes burdensome to everyone.
Children may feel relieved, rather than edified, when a long worship session ends. God is not honored if your family dreads the
time of Bible study and prayer. A short period of worship, on the
other hand, can stimulate the interest of each member and keep
him thinking about what was said.

Your Child from Birth to Rebirth by Anna B. Mow (Zondervan Publishing
House, 1976), pp. 30, 31.

Mark Twain once told about attending a church service where the minister preached on the need for generous giving. Twain was so impressed by the first ten minutes of the sermon that he pulled a twenty-dollar bill from his wallet. Ten minutes later the pastor was still talking, so Twain exchanged his twenty-dollar bill for a ten. Twenty minutes later Twain put the ten-dollar bill away and decided to take ten dollars out of the offering plate as it was passed! In our family worship, let's stop after those powerful first few minutes.

Do what your family enjoys doing. As you decide the length of your family worship, consider what best fits your family's "personality." Does your family love to gather around the piano and sing for twenty minutes every night? Or is a short, simple chorus about all the singing you care to do? Does your kindergartner pray for five minutes at a time, or does he have trouble saying a two-sentence prayer? Do you enjoy lengthy discussions and testimonies, or is your family reluctant to "open up" in this manner?

You must, of course, consider how much time family members have for spending on worship. Be realistic in this assessment if you plan to worship together on a regular basis. A retired couple might have 30 minutes or more to spend each day. On the other hand, a family, with husband and wife both working and with teenage children heavily involved in extra-curricular activities, might decide that a ten-minute worship period would best fit their schedules. Keep in mind, too, that your family will more likely "stick" with a short period of worship than a longer one.

Mini-worship while driving. What if you have only a small amount of time to spend together? What kind of worship experience would fit in with today's extra-hurried lifestyle? Several families I know have found that conversational worship around the dinner table can be very meaningful. The family members hold hands for prayer before the meal, signifying their love for each other and their unity before the Lord. Then, while they are eating, each in turn tells of how God has led in his life or of some blessing received during the day.

Another possibility when the family is really rushed for time—perhaps while riding in the car—is to have one member of the family offer prayer and then the entire family join in reciting a Bible text from memory. If time permits, a chorus such as "Spirit of the Living God" would enhance this brief gathering. You wouldn't want to make this sort of worship experience your daily fare just as you wouldn't want to live on snack foods. But you can certainly use this sort of mini-worship to help maintain the worship habit.

What about interruptions?

Interruptions to family worship will almost certainly occur, so develop a tentative plan for dealing with them. The most frequent interruption will probably be telephone calls. The simplest solution is to keep the phone off the hook during this time. Many families have instead decided to say, "We are having family worship now. Could you call back in half an hour?" This serves as a testimony both to the caller and, more importantly, to family members of the importance that you give to the worship of God.

Another possible interruption would be from guests who arrive unexpectedly. This is an excellent time to invite them to join you, to include them in your family's season of praise and fellowship.

How do you get started?

Hold a family council to plan worship. Once you have decided upon where and when to have worship and approximately how long it should be, how do you actually begin? Depending upon the ages of your children, you and your spouse will want to meet with them to plan your family altar. Let each person tell specifically how he wants to benefit from worship, what he would like to see included, and how he would like worship conducted.

This might include type of Bible study, method of prayer, the amount and type of singing, etc. (These areas will be discussed in detail in later sections.) You should also speak honestly about the difficulties you may encounter worshiping God together as a family: inhibition, lack of time, age differences, etc. This will encourage each member to take a personal interest and have a personal stake in the success of your "experiment" in worship.

Maybe you aren't quite ready to plunge directly into formal family worship and you need a preliminary step. If you do not feel comfortable about it, perhaps you can begin by discussing with other members of your family the wonderful things that God has done for you. This can be a short, spontaneous expression of your appreciation for some blessing. At first you might feel a bit self-conscious about saying, "The Lord really worked it out!" or "Jesus loves us so much. He even helped us find Spot." But soon it will come more naturally.

End the day with praise. This can prove a very effective witness not only to your family but also to your friends; soon everyone around you will be praising the Lord for His goodness. I have seen it happen in my family, and it can happen in yours!

Hindrances to family worship.

Even when you recognize all the abundant benefits of family worship, even when you give special time and attention to preparation, and even when you show extra enthusiasm for the worship session, certain factors will hinder your possibilities of success. Aside from the obvious liabilities of rushed schedules and lack of persistence in maintaining the worship time, there are some less obvious barriers to meaningful worship. Perhaps the chief two are fiction and television.

Distinguish between Bible truth and fiction. Anna Mow quotes a woman's recollections of her childhood experiences with God. Twice the woman mentions her Sunday school teacher, and each time she relates how the teacher combined the telling of Bible truth alongside fairy tales:

> My Sunday school teacher was a friend of Mother's. She told me the exciting stories of *Alice in Wonderland* and the *Wizard of Oz,* and the Sunday story was always about a little boy named Jesus.*

Later she refers to the teacher as "the fairy-tale lady who always told about the little boy Jesus on Sunday." Obviously the

---

*Your Child from Birth to Rebirth, p. 59.

woman carried this connection between truth and fiction until adulthood, long past the time when she rationally knew the difference.

When a child is very young, he believes everything he sees and hears. Anything can happen in a child's world of imagination, and probably will. At this time, it is very important that the child learns to discern between truth and fantasy. If he indiscriminately views the make-believe world of television cartoons and reads storybook fairy tales, he will mentally "catalogue" these images right beside his Bible stories.

This lesson was brought home to me vividly one night as I heard my daughter say to her doll, "You can go swimming in the river with Captain Naaman, but don't lie down and get your hair wet." Captain Naaman was as real to her as the neighbor across the street. And if she had seen Superman or Cinderella on television, they would have been equally as real.

Judiciously use fiction to illustrate truth. This doesn't mean that we can never use fiction to teach spiritual truth. After all, the Old Testament prophets used symbolism and Jesus used parables to convey their messages. Many classic fairy tales are fraught with Christian teaching. C. S. Lewis' Chronicles of Narnia present gospel truth with breath-taking imagination. We should not deprive our children of the rich lessons these stories offer. We should use them to full advantage, all the time reminding our children that these stories are just that—stories.

PART TWO

The Essentials of Family Worship

3. Prepare Your Own Heart

"These words, which I command thee this day, shall be in thine heart, and thou shalt teach them diligently" (Deut. 6:6, 7).

Before we can begin to teach our children, we must learn of God ourselves. Before we can instill in them a love of worship, we must love it ourselves. Before our children will give importance to Bible study and prayer, we ourselves must give it primary importance.

Maintain a personal walk with God. It seems only reasonable that the closer our walk with God, the more meaningful will be our family worship, whether it be adult worship or simple stories for children. We will have something special to impart—living experience with our Friend and Counselor, and revelation from His Spirit.

This has been especially evident in a prayer group I attend. The blessing the group receives seems to rise and fall according to the degree to which individual members spend time daily with the Lord. One day especially stands out because a group member had just learned to "wait on the Lord" for guidance in her life. She had presented her plans for the day to God, first thing in the morning. Then she remained on her knees for several minutes, waiting for God to tell her *His* plans for her. She finally received a specific answer to her prayer. God told her three things that she needed to work on immediately: be a better wife, spend more time with her mother, and return a coat that had been loaned to her daughter four years previous.

Somehow God's message about the coat struck a responsive chord in the hearts of the women in the group; we realized how much God cares, even about the little things of life. It was obvious that He had spoken directly to the woman—she had not even thought about the coat in six months.

After she related this experience to us, the group members each agreed to "wait on the Lord" during the following week for specific answers to prayer. Each woman returned to the next meeting with stories of God's rich blessings in her life.

Once you have prepared your own heart, it is time to focus on ways to make worship most meaningful to members of your family. We will consider the major aspects of worship in the following sections. Use these ideas as springboards to a worship time especially suited to your family.

4. Scripture

"Wherewithal shall a young man cleanse his way? by taking heed thereto according to thy word. With my whole heart have I sought thee: O let me not wander from thy commandments. Thy word have I hid in mine heart, that I might not sin against thee" (Ps. 119:9-11).

God's Word can be powerful in our lives. Surely no other book can point us to a better life, a richer, more meaningful existence. And even more amazing, it tells us *how* to do so.

Read Scripture as a fellow believer's testimony. But how do we unlock the treasures of the Bible? Too often our experience has been like that of Larry Christenson* and his family; they struggled for ten years, trying to establish and maintain meaningful Bible study and worship, but without success. They never gave up, though, and their persistence finally paid off. They discovered what Christenson considers the secret of effective Bible study: Instead of reading the Bible as a history book or some theological textbook, he and his family approached it as *a written account of a fellow believer's testimony of faith.* Instead of just "doing devotions," they began "receiving from a Christian brother a very personal account of his relationship with God.

Because Christenson had young children, he used Bible storybooks at first and then gradually began using the Gospels and the Old Testament. He read through the Bible very slowly,

---

The Christian Family by Larry Christenson (Bethany Fellowship, 1970).

perhaps only a few verses at a time. This way, the family could appreciate the depth of meaning hidden there.

The Christensons also interspersed actual Bible reading with written accounts from other "modern-day-believers." They read books such as, *The Jesus Family in Communist China* by Dr. Vaughan Rees and *The Cross and the Switchblade* by David Wilkerson. These present-day authors' accounts of Christian living added reality and relevance to the family's study of the Bible.

Not everyone agrees with Christenson's approach to Bible study. Some writers insist that the Bible itself be used for family worship instead of Bible storybooks—even for young children. They argue that one misses the beauty and majesty of the King James Version if he uses Bible storybooks or even modern translations of the Bible. Furthermore, many expressions from the King James Version are used in literature, and children will fail to recognize their origins if they are not familiar with this most commonly used version.

It is possible, also, that if we fail to use the Bible because we consider a child incapable of understanding it, the child may infer that the Bible must not be very important since we don't use it. On the other hand, we run the risk of discouraging a child's interest in family worship if we require him to sit quietly while we read from a book that he doesn't understand. He may thus infer that the Bible is a book we read but don't understand.

Read one verse and a corresponding story.

This dilemma requires good judgment on the part of all parents who seek to rear their children in "the nurture and admonition of the Lord." There are many possible courses of action between the extremes stated above. For very young children, perhaps one verse from the Bible will suffice, with an illustrated Bible storybook used to tell the story.

Tell the story, then read it.

Some families tell the Bible story in simple, but fascinating form for the younger children, then require the younger ones to sit quietly while the other members of the family read from the Bible itself. This training at home can teach children to sit quietly in church even though they don't fully understand the sermon. At the very least it can teach them a respect and reverence for the Word of God.

The types of Scripture suitable for different age groups will be covered in later chapters, but here are a few general ideas that can profit young and old alike. First, don't restrict your reading to one section of the Bible. Many people concentrate heavily on the four Gospels or the New Testament and neglect the fascinating accounts of God's dealings with people in the Old Testament. The Old Testament, after all, was the only Bible that Jesus or the early church had.

Try to relate the Old and New Testament to each other. Exodus and Hebrews both present the sacrificial systems instituted by God—in Exodus, as they pointed forward to Christ, and in Hebrews, as Christ himself became our sacrifice and High Priest. Daniel and Revelation both include prophecies about the end times. Many passages in Isaiah refer to the life of Christ as described in Matthew, Mark, Luke, and John.

Use Bible study guides. Second, use some resource material to make your Bible reading more meaningful. Tim LaHaye's *How to Study the Bible for Yourself** is an excellent guide to Bible study. It contains a three-year program which covers the entire Bible with strong emphasis on some of the more crucial chapters. It also contains a daily spiritual diary and numerous charts which will help the reader discover the key thoughts and concepts of Scripture.

Third, approach each Scripture reading with an open mind. You may have heard a passage many times throughout your life, but God is always able to give you new insights into what He is saying. Often teachers in the children's divisions at church complain that they are not being "fed" spiritually. Perhaps parents of small children have similar feelings, especially when they read the same story again and again (which is just what small children need and enjoy).

In these cases it is helpful for parents and teachers to take a fresh look at the Bible story they are relating, not only to help

---

*Harvest House Publishers, 1976.

overcome their boredom but to give greater understanding to the child. Consider, for instance, the account of the widow of Zarephath providing bread for Elijah when she and her son had almost nothing to eat. We generally tell this story to our children to teach them (1) to share, and (2) that God will take care of His children. We stress the miraculous multiplication of flour and oil.

<table>
<tr><td>Read Scripture to find "something new."</td><td>But what other lessons can we find in the experience of Elijah and the widow? Have you ever considered how hard it must have been for Elijah to humble himself enough to ask a widow (who was very poor) for bread, knowing that it was the very last loaf she and her son would have? Elijah must have found it very difficult to</td></tr>
</table>

obey God's command.

And what about the widow? Imagine what faith it took on her part to take bread—her final protection against starvation—away from her son and give it to a stranger! The thought must have crossed her mind, "What if this man is not a prophet of God? What if he is just trying to get my last bit of food so he won't starve? What if he tells this same story to everyone he meets?"

Another aspect of this Bible story holds a valuable lesson for youth and adults alike. God did not provide a new loaf of freshly baked bread every day for Elijah, the widow, and her son. Rather, He gave them only the meal and oil, and just enough for one day at that. No doubt Elijah (and possibly the son) had to gather wood for a fire while the widow stayed home and prepared the loaf. She could not make several loafs at one time, thus saving some work. She had to labor every day to provide food for the three of them.

God often deals with us like that. He gives us the "raw materials," but we must provide the effort. He freely gives us the Bible, His inspired Word, but we must study it for ourselves. He gives us free access to Him through prayer, but we must spend time on our knees. Often, too, He provides our needs just at the moment we need them and not before. If we do not trust Him, we will continually worry about tomorrow.

Read from a modern version. Fresh insights into such familiar Bible stories can often be gained by using a modern version or paraphrase of Scripture. The different vocabulary and sentence flow may be a key to unlocking exciting new insights.

Many families use family devotional books for their Bible study time. These often are made up of illustrative stories related to particular portions of Scripture. Many lead the readers to personal application, through the use of thought questions at the end of each story. A listing of such books is provided in the Appendix.

One final point about Bible study: *The Bible is God's Word.* He means for us to learn of Him through our study of Scripture, and He will help us learn. He has promised in Isaiah 55:10, 11: "For as the rain cometh down, and the snow from heaven, and returneth not thither, but watereth the earth, and maketh it bring forth and bud, that it may give seed to the sower, and bread to the eater: So shall my word be that goeth forth out of my mouth: it shall not return unto me void, but it shall accomplish that which I please, and it shall prosper in the thing whereto I sent it."

5. Prayer

Keep prayers short and specific.

Prayer during worship should be short and to the point: "Dear Father, please help Jimmy to remember what he's studied as he takes his geography test today. And please help Dad get along with Bill at the office, to be a good witness to his fellow workers." This is no time for lengthy discourses on the sinfulness of man or the plight of the heathen in faraway places.

Pray subject by subject.

Evelyn Christenson has given six very helpful suggestions on how to make your prayer life more meaningful in *What Happens When Women Pray:**

1. Pray subject by subject. While one person prays aloud about a particular topic, everyone else prays silently about the same thing. There is no planning of what you will say when your turn comes; rather, everyone prays unitedly, thus "multiplying the power of all the prayers that are ascending simultaneously to God's throne." As a variation of this, one person could pray a single sentence on a particular subject, followed by each family member praying a single sentence on the same topic.

2. Have short prayers. As mentioned earlier, short prayers are very much in order for family worship. Long prayers can make worship tiring, especially to young children, and may inhi-

---

*Victor Books, 1975.

bit the potential prayers of shy family members.

3. Have simple prayers. Simple prayers will also encourage the more timid and inexperienced family members to join in your prayer sessions.

Present specific prayer requests. 4. Have specific prayer requests. By praying about specific needs and problems, we can watch God at work. We can thus observe when and how He answers prayer, and our faith will increase as a result.

5. Have periods of silence. Prayer is a two-way conversation: we talk to God and He talks to us. But if we never take time to listen in silence for God's voice, how can we hear what He has to say? Spend part of your prayer time in silence—the length of time will depend to a great extent on the ages of your children and the amount of time you have set aside for worship. God will richly bless this quiet time.

6. Have small groups. Unless you have a large family, your prayer group will automatically be small. If, however, your family has six or more members, you might want to break up into groups of three to five persons.

Pray in various positions. For variety in prayer, your family might want to try different positions: sitting, standing, kneeling, holding hands, or even prostrate as did Jacob when he wrestled with the angel. Use these various positions only if they add meaning to your prayer times.

There are also several methods of praying that you might like to try. Probably the most typical method, but not necessarily the most effective, is to have one member of the family (usually Father) pray aloud while everyone else remains silent.

Other families let each member pray in turn, from the smallest toddler up to Grandmother and Granddad. This has the advantage of letting each person talk with God, but it may make some family members feel uncomfortable.

A variation of the each-member-prays method, and one that seems to appeal to many people, is conversational prayer. Here one person begins prayer with just a sentence or two; then someone else (not necessarily the next person in line) says a short

46

prayer, preferably on the same subject. The
group continues in this way, with everyone praying as he desires to do so. Eventually a few moments of silence will indicate that the season of
prayer is over.

Have conversa-tional prayer.

A fourth type of prayer allows each person to
pray silently at the same time on the same subject. The prayer
leader asks all family members to pray for something specific:
"Please pray that Aunt Sue's operation will be successful";
"Now ask God to forgive you for some particular sin you may
have committed today."

This type of prayer can be especially meaningful because
everyone prays at the same time; there is no waiting around
while someone else is praying. Also, there is less opportunity for
one's mind to wander, and no one feels uncomfortable should he
not want to pray aloud.

Praise aloud together.

A fifth method of prayer is one which should
be used carefully, but can be nonetheless very
useful for praise. This method is taken from the
interpretation that some Christians give to Acts
4:24: "They lifted up their voice to God with one accord." The
implication is that these people all prayed aloud—at once! This
practice is definitely not for the self-conscious, but it can stimulate exuberant praise.

Keep a prayer notebook.

Several authors suggest that one keep a
prayer notebook noting prayer requests, the date
praying began and the date the prayer was answered. This helps reinforce in everyone's mind
that God does answer prayer. This, of course,
takes a large measure of faith on the part of parents. What happens if no answer is apparent? How does one explain this to the
children? Larry Christenson has examined this dilemma and
concluded:

> All too often we fail to lead our children into simple ventures
> of faith because we are afraid to lay our own faith on the line. Be-
> hind our pious pretensions lurks the fear, "What if nothing hap-
> pens?" Well, what if nothing *does* happen? If God is not a prayer-
> answering God, aren't we better off to find it out right now, and

have done with this pious nonsense? If God can't be approached with our everyday needs, aren't we better off to discover it right now, so that our children can be spared the hypocrisy and futility of believing in an all-powerful God who never lifts a finger?

Oftentimes prayers are *not* answered. And let us not take refuge in the pious assertion that He *always* answers, but sometimes the answer is "No" or "Wait." This little pat on the head is intended to hold faith unshaken. But actually it reduces prayer to an impersonal exercise in doctrine, rather than a living encounter with God. It is altogether true that sometimes God *does* say "No." But that "No" is not simply the logical inference which we draw when our prayer goes unanswered. It is an actual experience which yields to us the assurance that God has spoken—just as blessed, in its own way, as a resounding "Yes." But often we experience neither a "Yes" nor a "No"—just a silence. We must have the courage to venture with our children into these waters that test our faith. For it is here that we learn how to pray aright. It is here that we wrestle with God until He blesses us. It is here that the encounter with God becomes real. Unanswered prayer is like an unsuccessful experiment—a spur to further research.*

If parents and children undertake this faith experiment, if they test God to see if He really cares about them, He will not disappoint them. He has promised, "Then shalt thou call, and the Lord shall answer; thou shalt cry, and he shall say, Here I am" (Isa. 58:9). He will answer all who seek Him diligently, earnestly, and persistently.

Larry Christenson also suggested several different prayer projects. Your family might want to use a different one each day or try one type of prayer for a whole week at a time.

1. *The prayer of faith.* Let each member choose a prayer objective that he knows is God's will. Jesus never said to a leper, "Be clean if it is God's will." He knew what God wanted and so should we—through Bible study, meditation, and prayers for guidance.

Your prayer objective might be to have calmness and confidence when you make a speech to a certain group. It might be to have God heal an ill friend or that Granddad recognize Jesus'

The Christian Family (pp. 152, 153.)

48

love for him. Whatever the objective, picture in your mind God accomplishing your request. Imagine yourself not shaking in fright, but calm and confident during your speech. Visualize your friend in the best of health or Granddad rejoicing over new-found knowledge of Christ.

Then tell God about the visual image you see (e.g., "Dear Father, send your Holy Spirit to Granddad to fill his heart with your love. Show him in some special way how much you care for him."). Finally, give thanks that God has answered your prayer in the way He knows is best.

2. *Prayer for the family.* Let each person choose a certain relative or member of the immediate family and pray for some need that the person has.

Use the Lord's Prayer creatively.

3. *The Lord's Prayer.* You may repeat the prayer together or have Father say the prayer, one sentence at a time, after which family members make specific applications of the general sentence. If Father prays, "Give us this day our daily bread," Mother might ask that they find a way to pay for the new tires they need, and Sister might pray for wisdom to learn geometry.

4. *Prayer for missionaries and church leaders.* Designate a particular person or family and pray for them. This will help your family feel part of the worldwide church.

5. *Prayer of confession.* Let each person confess some act or habit that has disturbed family harmony. After the confession, all other family members should express forgiveness, then pray for God to help the person overcome this particular sin. This can foster understanding and family unity if done in the right spirit.

Pray for national leaders.

6. *Prayer for our nation's leaders.* In these times of great international unrest, our leaders can certainly use our prayers for God's strength and wisdom.

7. *Prayer for the church.* Pray for the church *you* attend, not the worldwide church which was covered under #4. Let each member pray for some aspect of church life: the youth program, nursing home visitation, the Sunday school, the pastor, individuals in need.

8. *Prayer for guidance.* This prayer, which often precedes the prayer of faith, asks God to reveal His will in a particular situation. It begins with a period of silent waiting as you prepare your heart to receive God's direction. Once you are quiet, inwardly and outwardly, ask God to show you His will. Willingly accept what God tells you, no matter what it is. Then thank God for revealing His way to you, obey, then wait for the exciting results.

9. *Prayer of adoration.* This prayer praises God for His goodness, mercy, power, wisdom. Its purpose is to move your attention from yourself to God. This will open up your heart to His presence.

10. *Prayer of meditation.* This is primarily a quiet time spent in the presence of God. Visualize God upon His throne, the face of Jesus, or a word or phrase to keep your mind from wandering. Your main purpose is simply to enjoy the presence of God.

11. *Prayer of intercession.* In this prayer you pray for someone else with a need. Imagine before you pray that you are taking this person into yourself. Thus you become intimately involved with the prayed-for person and are much less likely to be judgmental or critical. In essence you become a mediator between God and the other person, allowing God to deal with the need or problem.

Study prayer in the Bible. As a final note: conduct a Bible study on the subject of prayer. Read one or all of the following chapters of Scripture: 1 Kings 8; Psalms 42, 51; Luke 11:1-13; 18:1-14; John 17, and Ephesians 3.

6. Music

You will have a wide variety of modes of music to choose from for family worship: anything from a cappella singing to Mom at the piano, Dad on the guitar, and the children with rhythm instruments. You will be limited, of course, by the musical instruments available in your home as well as by the musical talent represented. But don't overlook some less-than-obvious ways to "make a joyful noise unto the Lord."

Allow everyone to play an instrument. Search for worship-enhancing music right in your own family. Does any member of the family play a musical instrument, even just simple melodies? This person could play a solo or accompany group singing. The instrument might be a piano, guitar, recorder, or saxophone; it really doesn't matter as long as the music is uplifting and reverent. A father I know plays three or four songs on his guitar every evening while his wife and children sing along. This not only delights his family but gives him incentive to develop his playing ability.

Young children love rhythm instruments: bells, triangles, sticks, drums. By all means let them play these instruments while the family sings; it will greatly heighten their interest by making them feel a part of the worship format. But remember that we are teaching reverence and love for the Lord, so don't let the young musicians get out of hand. "Let all things be done decently and in order" (1 Cor. 14:40).

Younger members of the family will also enjoy a song which prepares their hearts and minds for prayer. First try the ones your children sing at church; this will direct their thoughts to a setting associated with Jesus and His worship. After-prayer songs are very meaningful also. Your family might like singing "Into My Heart" or, for variety, they might like humming "Blest Be the Tie That Binds."

Perform a "Bible opera." Children of five or older enjoy Bible story musicals in which children and parents play different characters from the Bible. For example, you might re-enact Christ's feeding the multitude. You could use as many characters as you have family members: Christ, the boy with the loaves and fishes, the disciples and hungry people in the crowd. Each actor makes up words and music for his character as the "opera" progresses. Everybody not only has lots of fun, but also develops a deeper understanding and "feel" for the Bible story. These narratives come alive as each family member becomes personally involved.

Sing Scripture choruses. Many adults and children have had great success memorizing Bible verses by putting them to music. This facilitates the learning process as well as making it much more fun. Make up your own tunes for the simpler verses ("Sing unto the Lord" was the first I tried; it seemed especially appropriate.).

For longer portions of Scripture, purchase an inexpensive book with Psalms and other sections of the Bible set to music. I have enjoyed *Sing the Word** by Carolyn Bisel and Dan Klein. Once you have learned the music and words, you'll find yourself singing these songs throughout the day as you work, walk, or drive. The habit will bless you as well as your family and associates.

The housekeeper who worked for us when I was growing up

*Write: Gymnics Sing the Word, Department of Physical Education, Andrews University, Berrien Springs, Michigan 49104.

Also recommended: *Songs for Christian Folk*, vol. 1 & 2, by Gary Johnson (Bethany House Publishers); *The Singing Word,* Mary Warrington, ed. (© Jugend mit einer Mission e.V., dist. by Bethany House Publishers).

had a beautiful alto voice. She would arrive for work every Monday morning singing, "This is my story, this is my song; praising my Savior all the day long. . . ." Apparently she sang it every Sunday in her church choir and just kept right on singing into the work week.

I loved that song as a child and still love it, no doubt because every time I sing or hear it, I think of our wonderful Christian housekeeper. And, amazingly enough, this is my daughter's favorite hymn. She heard it once when we had worship at a friend's home and has been singing it ever since. God uses these songs about His love to lift our thoughts toward Him.

Learn a new song each week. Larry Christenson relates that he purchased inexpensive songbooks—one for each family member—to use daily in worship. The family chose a different song every week to sing at the beginning of worship. The children tended to select familiar hymns while the parents often tried an unfamiliar one. The family, over the years, acquired a broad repertoire of Christian music, one song at a time. A person who has grown up in a singing family and church can thumb through a hymnal and recognize probably 300-400 hymns and choruses!

Relate songs to Bible lessons. Whatever music you choose, be sure your songs relate to lessons you are teaching. Children love to sing "The Wise Man Built His House upon a Rock," but unless they understand the spiritual lesson it illustrates, it will do little more than entertain them. On the other hand, if you read the parable in the Bible or tell them the story in your own words, explaining the lesson Jesus was illustrating, then this song will be very meaningful and appropriate for worship.

7. Dialogue

Psychologists have discovered an interesting principle of learning: the amount of information one retains depends to a large extent on his degree of participation in the learning process. They have found, for instance, that a person learns ten percent of what he *reads*, twenty percent of what he *hears*, thirty percent of what he *sees*, fifty percent of what he *says*, and ninety percent of what he *says and does*.

These findings have important implications for the type of worship we have in our homes. The idea that worship should consist of a family sitting quietly while Father reads the Scripture has obvious drawbacks. There needs to be participation of some kind among all the family members.

Discuss personal experiences. Discussion of experiences or insights related to the Bible study topic personally involves family members in the worship time. They not only *say* something about the topic but they indirectly *do* something, for as they recount an event, they mentally relive it; they "do" it again. Such a personal point of view can be much more meaningful to other family members than an illustration or anecdote given by an unseen and unknown author of a devotional book.

Several generations of our family met one night with a church elder for a prayer service. He read the prescribed literature and had a closing prayer. Just as everyone was preparing to adjourn, one member asked a pertinent question about what was read.

Soon everyone joined in, trying to add further light to the subject. When the group finally dismissed, everyone had confessed his deep need of the Lord and had rededicated his life to Him. An evening of perfunctory reading and listening had been transformed into a vibrant celebration of spiritual renewal. What made the difference? The *active* involvement of each group member relating the evening's reading to his personal life.

Illustrate truth with experience. Even if his group is not very responsive, the worship leader can add his own personal comments and thereby bring an abstract spiritual concept into sharp focus for everyday living. When my husband and I were being interviewed for his first teaching position, we had the privilege of attending family worship with one of the college faculty members. We gathered with the man and his family just before breakfast in a family room. A fire glowed and crackled in the fireplace.

In this lovely setting, he read about our need to obey principle, whether or not others are aware of our actions and whether or not our actions will affect others. He then cemented this thought in our minds with an illustration from his own life.

One morning he was out driving so early that he saw no other cars. He came to a stop sign and almost ignored it because he knew that no other car would possibly be coming. Suddenly he realized that he should stop, even if it seemed a needless ritual, because every action one takes is helping to form a habit, good or bad. He reasoned that if he intentionally ignored the stop sign then, when he knew it would do no harm, it might increase his likelihood of mistakenly ignoring it later.

Five years later, I still remember that illustration. It is extremely doubtful that I would have remembered the subject of that morning worship if the leader had not delved into his personal experiences for an illustration of the day's lesson.

Family members who feel comfortable unveiling personal problems and temptations open the way for the Lord to work powerfully in their lives. God tells us to "confess your faults one to another, and pray one for another, that ye may be healed" (James 5:16). When we reveal our innermost need to our family, we will often find that other members have experienced or are experiencing the same trial and need we face. We are then able to support each other.

One day I went to my weekly prayer group with a deep concern about my spiritual condition. My personal devotions were becoming shorter. They were also being held closer and closer to bedtime when I could barely stay awake. Of course, there was a "reason"—Satan always has a plentiful supply of these—but I knew that God would help me take more time for my devotional life if I would just let Him have control.

As our group knelt and prayed, I was amazed to hear another group member telling God of this very same problem in her life. How comforting it was to know that I was not alone! Together we could believe that God had the power to draw both of us back to Him through daily worship. At the end of the prayer group session, this other member and I made a covenant between ourselves and God that we would spend at least fifteen minutes a day with Him.

Make covenants with each other. When family members freely confess their faults in this manner, they provide a wonderful opportunity for making covenants. Imagine the wonderful effects if Brother and Sister covenanted to not insult each other for a month. And imagine what would happen if Father and Son covenanted to spend one hour each Saturday talking about their problems. Family relationships would be transformed!

Divulge your highs and lows. Outside the realm of formal worship, you can also use the techniques of dialogue very effectively. This is one of the best ways to teach you children how to walk with God. Talk about your spiritual highs and lows with your child *as they happen*. They will gain spiritual insights almost firsthand as they live through trials and victories with you. This technique will also teach them to take their problems to the Lord. They will see how God answers prayer, both for them and for others.

8. Visual Aids

Visual aids can make the diffence between blasé, irrelevant narrative and a fascinating, vivid retelling of an event in the life of a Bible character. One Sunday afternoon I was telling my two-year-old daughter about the Apostle Peter's miraculous release from prison. She was extremely fascinated by the chains on Peter's wrists and ankles. I therefore seached for some real chains she could hold, thus making the story more meaningful. In the corner of the garage lay the chains we mounted on the tires of our snow plow. As I gazed at them, suddenly the story became more meaningful to *me*. Those chains must have scraped Peter's wrists and ankles raw. His arms and legs must have ached and cramped. Peter's suffering came alive to me, and I was better able to tell it to my daughter.

Make a "worship box."

There are many kinds of visual aids: pictures, felts, stick-on art, finger plays, maps, figurines, etc. Use a variety of these (depending, of course, on the age of your children) to keep worship time a much-anticipated event. One family I know has a "worship box" with at least two each of several different items. Included are bells, flowers, butterflies and small stuffed animals to be used in conjunction with various worship songs and stories. If another child (or adult) visits the family, he has a device to use, too. The little boy in this family loves his worship time so much that he always reminds his parents when it is time for worship, even if they are visiting in another home.

Pictures are especially helpful for very small children. Make a "My Angel Cares for Me" book. Attach one angel at the top of each page and pictures underneath of your child engaged in various activities: sleeping, eating, playing, bathing. He will love to hear how his angel cares for him all the time, especially when you've made it so personal with his own pictures.

Compile a family scrapbook. Consider making a family scrapbook with a similar theme. Illustrate how Jesus loves your youngster so much that He gave him a family. Use pictures of parents, siblings, grandparents and other relatives.

Purchase one set of modern-day people and one set of Bible people to depict Bible stories. Either set will help teach Bible truths to children. Visual impact is tremendously effective!

Older children will enjoy painting or drawing pictures to illustrate the worship topic. This may be done during worship or at some other time. If the drawing is related to the topic of worship, the Bible lesson will be cemented in the child's mind.

Use lifelike visual aids. Use visual aids that are lifelike as possible. Use realistic stuffed animals, for they will make a stronger impression than pictures or felts. Use silk flowers or real flowers cut from the garden. Use real fruit from the kitchen instead of artificial fruit or pictures.

Christmas is an especially good time for realistic visual aids. Many families use a manger scene, or crèche, as a holiday decoration. Take time to talk to your child about the birth of Jesus, showing him the different figures. Perhaps you can find a life-sized nativity scene in your community to which to take your child. This would be most meaningful to him.

You are likely to tell the same Bible story over and over again to small children. Therefore, it is a good idea to use different visual aids each time. This will hold their interest and add variety to your worship. For instance, if you are telling about Creation and how God made the animals, one day you might use felts, the second day pictures, the third day small toy animals (let a child close his eyes and pick one out of a bag), the fourth day stuffed animals, and the fifth day dramatization (let the children pretend they are the different animals God has created). They will learn the lesson well and won't be bored by the repetition of the same material.

Play Bible charades. Play Bible charades with children of almost any age above two. Younger children can act out simple stories while you narrate them (Daniel in the lions' den, David and Goliath, etc.). As the children get older, they can pantomime scenes from the Bible while you try to guess what they are portraying.

Enhance Bible stories with maps. Maps are an excellent visual aid for older children. As the family reads about Christ's journeying to and fro in the Holy Land, follow His route on a map. As you note the terrain He covered and the distances from one city to another, Christ's life will become more real to you. Use maps, also, when studing about Abraham's travels, Israel's wanderings, and Paul's missionary journeys.

9. Make It Special

What are your child's two favorite days of the year? Probably, they are Christmas and his birthday. You spend time and effort preparing for these days. You make special foods, put up appropriate decorations, and buy and wrap gifts. You spend hours, days, weeks—even months—getting ready. What would Christmas be like this year if you woke up on December 25 and thought, "Well, today's Christmas. I'd better throw together a few things so we can celebrate!" Christmas and birthdays require preparation to make them special and so does family worship.

Adapt topics to specific needs. One of the simplest ways to make worship special for your family is to gear the topic of study to a need someone is experiencing at that time. Search the Scriptures together for guidelines for your particular situation.

Does Brother feel mistreated or misunderstood by his teachers at school? David wrote scores of Psalms describing these same feelings and God's solution for them.

Does Father have a problem with impetuousness or anger? Study the lives of impulsive Peter or John, the "sons of thunder," and see how Christ transformed these traits.

Is Mother concerned about "how the bills will be paid this month"? Read Christ's descriptions of God's love for us and His provision of our earthly needs (Luke 12:22-31).

The style of worship should reflect your family's personality.

In a family of musicians, for instance, singing or playing instruments could be emphasized. This might even culminate in the family's playing for public performances.

Sometimes a special trait of your family can add spice to worship time. A friend of mine, the mother of two small daughters, has used family worship as a means of passing on her cultural heritage. Her parents came to America from Germany right before she was born, so she grew up with a strong German influence in her home.

As a girl and young woman, she sang German songs during her family's worship time. She was often embarrassed when friends came to visit during worship and heard these German songs. But when her husband-to-be first heard this "family-worship, German-style," he was delighted with it. He even encouraged his future wife to incorporate some German songs into their own family worship. Now they gather every morning and evening to sing, praise, and pray—and half their songs and prayers are in English and half are in German. Their three-year-old twins can sing several German songs and can even pray in German.

Use nature's object lessons. Use nature extensively to illustrate truths and to "spice up" worship times. The Bible has been called God's first book and nature His second. The beauty of His creation, though marred by sin, can give us a deeper appreciation and love for our Creator. It can also provide spiritual lessons; even Christ used elements of nature—the lily, the fig tree—to teach us about God.

Be alert for biblical references to natural phenomena your children see frequently. When you read about the leaven of the Pharisees, make bread with your children and show them how a teaspoon of yeast permeates the whole loaf. When you read of Christ's describing His people as the "salt of the earth; but if the salt have lost his savour, wherewith shall it be salted?" (Matt. 5:13), leave salt out of your next meal. Your children will vividly understand and remember Christ's lesson.

Go outdoors and study Jesus' parables from nature. For instance, if the parable is of the sower and the seeds, first read and

Worship
outdoors.
study the lesson outside on a blanket. Then search around the yard or neighborhood or even visit a farm to find the different types of soil described. If the season is right, plant seeds in the fertile soil and watch their growth over the months. During winter months, you could sprout seeds indoors.

When you, your child, or your family look closely at God's handiwork in nature, you will gain a new appreciation for the Creator's imagination, wisdom, and power. Consider, for example, how the world would look if God had made everything one color—gray. The sky would be gray, the trees, flowers, birds, and grass would be gray. How then could we possibly imagine a red apple, blue eyes, or a purple sunset? This would be beyond our finite capacity, just as it is impossible now for us to imagine a color which is not a combination or shade of the ones we already know.

Or consider God's sense of humor in the variety of animals He made: He created some animals like cats and dogs with "standard equipment." But He didn't stop there. The elephant received a very long nose, the giraffe a very long neck, the kangaroo very big feet, the alligator a very big mouth.

Take time with your family to examine closely some of God's handiwork. Collect insects or wild flowers and present your discoveries at family worship on a special night, say, once a week. Worship outside, under the stars, on a crisp fall night. Being outside under the vast starry sky makes me feel very small, but very thankful, that the God who created and rules the universe also cares for me. This setting is ideal for fostering reverence and a worship spirit.

Worship at
unusual
places.
Don't forget special places for worship, either: on the beach, atop a mountain, at your favorite lake or river, in a secluded cave. These times can give you and your family vivid memories of time spent with God. I remember a program on Creation that I saw with my family at Natural Bridge, Virginia, about twenty years ago. The program was held outside at night, with different colored lights shining on the various rock formations. The narration came from the first few chapters of

Genesis. I sensed a closeness to God then that returns whenever I recall that evening. Memories like this can be yours as well.

Occasionally you will want to do something really out of the ordinary for worship. The ideas that follow are more dramatic than most you will use every day; their purpose is to make the Bible and spiritual lessons "come alive" for your family. They are, for the most part, the living out of spiritual truths. With some preparation on your part, they can make a tremendous impact on your family.

Celebrate your spiritual birthday.

1. One of the best ideas I've heard is to make spiritual birthdays very special events. Anyone can tell you the day he was born, but how many people can tell you the day they were born again into God's family, the day they accepted Christ? We can make this event stand out by celebrating it with as much enthusiasm as we do a physical birthday. When a family member's spiritual birthday rolls around, hold a banquet and invite several friends. If the family budget allows, let the one celebrating purchase a new outfit to wear. At the banquet have special prayer, thanking the Lord for the spiritual birthday and asking His blessing during the coming year. This annual occasion will stress how important the family considers its commitment to Christ.

Build an altar of special experiences.

2. Study the children of Israel's crossing of the Jordan. Recount how they gathered stones from the riverbed and with them built an altar to commemorate God's miraculous parting of the Jordan. Then let members of your family begin their own stone altars in the backyard. Have each stone represent one very special experience with God: a direct answer to prayer, a special blessing, the conversion of a friend or family member. The adding of each new stone could be either a personal or a family event, but in either case it should be a highly meaningful ritual.

3. On December 31, have every family member write his spiritual objectives for the coming year. Pray, asking God to help each member accomplish his objectives, then have everyone seal his paper in a bottle and bury it. The bottles can be dug up the

following December 31 so that everyone can evaluate his spiritual progress. (In northern areas where the ground freezes, a more practical place to "bury" them might be way in the back of the basement closet.)

4. A family I know erected a tent of blankets in one corner of their living room while they were studying Abraham's life. The people each wore brightly colored robes for worship every evening.

5. Read the story of the widow giving her mites. Then establish a self-denial box where family members put money that they would have spent on luxuries (candy, new clothes, eating out, etc.). Send the money to a relief agency.

6. Let older children write a play to present to relatives on a special occasion, such as a birthday. Have a meal together, then have the children perform. Use props and simple costumes. Adam and Eve could be dressed in white sheets with flashlights underneath to represent their garments of righteousness. After the Fall they could wear green clothes with leaves tacked on.

7. Have a talent night, one night each week or month, when each family member will present a special part of the worship. One person might read an original poem, another play music, a third sing a song, another draw a mural depicting some Bible scene.

8. Have a Bible feast for your children and their friends. Let them eat in a special place, perhaps outside on a blanket in the summer or in front of the fireplace in the winter. Serve special foods—not necessarily fancy but some your children really enjoy. Sing favorite songs and have candles burning. After the meal, turn out all the lights and tell Bible stories by candlelight. Memorable!

9. Study about Hannah dedicating Samuel to live in the temple and serve God. Then let each family member covenant to serve God for a day, week, or month in some special way: visit shut-ins, do home repairs for an elderly person in the neighborhood, etc. If the covenant is for a week, light a candle for each day that has passed. On the last day, have a praise service in which everyone tells of the blessing he has received from serving others.

Give hand-made gifts to each other.

10. Have a Mary Magdalene night in which each person gives something special to other family members: pressed flowers, pictures, plants, homemade pastries. This is to commemorate Mary Magdalene's gift of spikenard to Christ, showing Him her love and devotion. The emphasis should be on something made rather than bought. (This might also be used when studying about the boy who gave the loaves and fishes to Christ.)

Take a "journey of love."

11. Several years ago a major woman's magazine suggested that its readers take a "journey of love." The first week: *The Hand of Love.* Write a letter to a close friend, telling how much he is appreciated.

The second week: *The Voice of Love.* Telephone several people each day to say, "Thank You," "I'm sorry," or "You mean a lot to me," or just to get better acquainted.

The third week: *The Deed of Love.* Take small gifts to several people who are very special to you: plants, home-baked pies, potholders, etc.

The fourth week: *The Heart of Love.* Make a prayer list of at least ten people: friends, relatives, enemies. Pray for them daily. Make peace with those you've wronged or who have wronged you.

The fifth week: *The Mind of Love.* Read the gospel of John. Carefully examine your own life and pray for areas of need.

The sixth week: *The Victory of Love.* Celebrate God's goodness to you. Take time to go outside and breathe the fresh air. Invite friends over for dinner. Reflect on how God has blessed you during your "journey of love."

Celebrate a "Heavenly Festival."

12. Celebrate a "Heavenly Festival," representing what life will be like in heaven. To attend, each person must say the password: "Jesus is my Savior," "Jesus took my sins away," etc. If your children are old enough to understand this concept, don't tell them the password in advance. Have everyone wear white robes (sheets) and crowns. Drink the "water

of life" and eat fruit from the "tree of life." Prepare whatever foods you consider appropriate for the Marriage Supper of the Lamb. Let Father take a napkin and "wipe away all tears from their eyes."

PART THREE

Something for Everyone

10. Never Too Early, Never Too Late

Barb sat happily in the large, comfortable chair, surrounded by baby blankets, sleepers, booties, and diapers. Friends were giving her a baby shower; her first child was due in just a few weeks. The large rectangular box, much heavier than the others, intrigued her. What could it possibly be?

At last she opened it and found inside a large-print Bible with many beautiful pictures. The note attached to it read, "For use in your family altar." Barb laughingly remarked, "Well, it'll be a long time before I'll be able to have family worship with the new baby."

The friend who had given her the Bible wisely responded, "Are you going to wait a long time before you begin to feed the baby?"

"Well, no," Barb replied.

"Then don't wait to start feeding your baby the Word of God, either."

Include your infant in worship. Barb had learned a valuable lesson. Not only would she begin having worship right away with her baby, but she would also make the worship suitable for his age level. She would begin feeding her new baby warm milk, later introducing cereals, soft foods, then a complete diet; similarly, she would begin with a very simple, basic worship format, later adding more complex lessons as the child grew and matured.

The first few years of a child's life are crucial. During this time he develops habits and attitudes which he will carry throughout his lifetime. This is the time to build a strong foundation for future Christian growth.

Sing about Jesus to your baby. During these early years, a child can *experience* love and *experience* Christ and then associate these two concepts. This is far more important than formal teaching. As a mother rocks her baby and holds him close, she should softly sing about Jesus and His love. As she lets Baby stroke the kitten's fur, she should tell how Jesus made the kitten. As she lets him smell a rose, she should speak the name of Jesus. Gradually the child associates the name of Jesus with life's most pleasant experiences.

Associate Jesus with pleasant experiences. Even if you have failed to provide your child with family worship during the crucial first years, you need not despair. God will bless your efforts, no matter when and where you start. Consider the story of Brother Leonard, a missionary to India:

His parents were artists and they had both grown tired of being considered different because they were Jewish. They decided that their son should not have to go through life as they had, and so, when Leonard was eight they sent him to a Christian boarding school. They told the teachers that Leonard was to be treated and taught just like the boys from Christian families. He was not to think of himself as being different.

For the first time Leonard heard the stories of Jesus. Each day passages from the gospels were read in school without comment. It wasn't long until Jesus became his hero. He looked forward eagerly each day to the time for Scripture reading. When Leonard was thirteen the rest of his group entered a confirmation class. When the Jewish lad found out that this was preparation for becoming a disciple of Jesus, he was delighted beyond measure! He hadn't realized before that such a thing was possible. But the headmaster of the school, fearing this was going too far, told Leonard they would have to get his parents' permission. The parents were stunned. They hadn't counted on anything like this, but they didn't want to spoil the fellowship their son had

had in this school he loved so much. After serious consideration they decided he was *only* thirteen and he would surely soon forget this experience when he went on to other schools, so they gave their permission for Leonard to become a Christian.

The boy was delighted and he was a most studious and eager pupil as he learned what it meant to be a Christian. Then he was baptized and he took his first communion. Some twenty years later when he told me this story in India he added with great warmth: "Before that communion Jesus was my hero, but in some way I cannot yet explain, as I took communion, Jesus, my hero, became Jesus, my Saviour. I knew His living presence. He holds me to this day."*

It is never too late to begin!

But no matter what your child's age, you should adapt family worship to his needs. Just as the farmer varies his tasks according to the maturity of his crops, so the parent must vary worship according to his child's age and ability. The farmer must prepare the soil, plant the seeds, till the ground, and kill the weeds before he gathers the harvest. Likewise, the wise parent will teach his children to love and reverence God one step at a time. The following sections will give you basic ideas for worship at different stages in your child's development.

*Your Child from Birth to Rebirth, pp. 166-167.

11. Birth Through Six Months

Pray for your baby before birth.

How do you tell a tiny baby about Jesus? How do you begin? And when? If you wait until your child is born to start preparing him for a life with Christ, you have already missed a golden opportunity to direct his spiritual life. As soon as a husband and wife learn that they are expecting a baby, they should begin praying for that tiny life that is rapidly developing. They can pray every day that the Holy Spirit will rest on the growing child, making him responsive to God's leading and receptive to the spiritual instruction he will receive later on. They should also ask for wisdom to lead that child to the Lord.

Once a baby is born, he experiences life outside the warmth and security of his mother's womb. How he views the world—as loving and accepting, or as hostile and rejecting—will greatly affect his later learning and experiences. If he feels loved, he can more readily believe that God loves him. If he can trust his parents to care for his every need, he can more readily trust God for provision. The most important thing parents can do during the first year of life is to love their baby and *help him to know that he is loved.*

This seems so obvious that we could easily pass over this idea with a glib, "Well, of course I love my baby and of course he knows it!" But it's not always that obvious to him. In *I Ain't Much Baby, but I'm All I've Got,* Jess Lair describes the feelings

72

of worthlessness and pain many people experience because they didn't feel loved as children. He maintains that nearly every person, if honest, would admit to these same feelings. The child perceives that "all is not well" between himself and his parents, that something must be wrong either with the parents or with him. When he sees how powerful, knowledgeable, and large his parents are, he concludes that the fault must lie with him.

What can a Christian parent do to prevent this from happening to his child? Dr. Ross Campbell suggests that although most parents do love their children, they don't know how to communicate this love to their child. The *feeling* of love does not get through.

Show love through eye contact. Dr. Campbell has discovered three basic methods by which we can *show* our children how much we love them. The first method is *eye contact*. We must look at our children, looking directly into their eyes, when we are interacting with them. A tiny baby, barely able to focus, will turn his head from side to side, searching for another pair of eyes to look at. So all children, from birth on, need to know that we love them enough, that they are worthwhile enough, for us to take the time to look directly at them.

Show love through physical contact. A second method is *physical contact*. We need to hold, cuddle, and kiss our children when they are are babies and toddlers. As they grow, our methods of giving physical affection will change, but contact must always be there.

Physical contact is relatively easy to give to babies; their very natures demand it. We carry them from place to place; we generally hold them while feeding them. During the years of later childhood and adolescense, physical contact suffers neglect. Many parents feel uncomfortable hugging or kissing their nearly-grown children. Unfortunately, they don't change methods of physical contact; instead, they give it up altogether.

Dr. Campbell suggests that parents of older children use a pat on the shoulder, a handshake, or playful wrestling as means of expressing love. They must continue *some* form of appropriate physical contact.

74

Show love through focused attention.

A third method of showing love to our children is *focused attention.* This means that we stop everything we are doing when we interact with our child one-to-one. If he wants to talk, we listen intently; we don't think about some task we need to do. If he wants to paint, we enter wholeheartedly into the painting; we don't paint with our hands while our minds plan tomorrow's shopping list.

Full attention is the highest compliment one person can pay another. Consider how *you* feel when you are talking to someone who is not paying full attention. He may pretend to be listening, but you know he is just being polite. This can make you feel rather unimportant.

Now consider a time when your spouse or close friend talked with you about some problem or idea; if he really involved himself in the discussion, asking just the right questions that let you know he cared, you no doubt felt deeply satisfied after the encounter. This is the very experience you should give your child. It leaves him feeling loved and worthwhile—a feeling he won't find anywhere else.

Begin giving focused attention when the child's a tiny baby. Breast-feeding, for example, can provide very positive physical contact for a baby, and usually for the mother as well. A woman can breast-feed her baby while watching TV, reading a book, or even cooking supper. But if she does so, she focuses no attention on the child and his "love tank" may run a bit low. How rewarding it would be for her and the child if she set aside everything else she might do and just interacted with her baby, verbally or nonverbally, as she nursed him.

Giving love in these ways takes a lot of time, a commodity that seems harder to come by every day. But consider what eye contact, physical contact, and focused attention can do for your child, both emotionally and spiritually. This will inspire you to find (or make) the necessary time.

While an infant, your child doesn't have the *intellectual* capacity to understand about Jesus. He learns everything *experientially.* He can therefore learn about Jesus only as you speak His name with love, joy, and reverence. Do talk to your child

Speak lovingly of Jesus. about Jesus. Tell him how much Jesus loves him, always remembering that *what* you say isn't nearly as important as *how* you say it.

When conducting worship with your infant, you primarily are giving impressions and experiences rather than information. The baby learns by absorption; he "soaks in" intuitive concepts of love, a prayerful spirit, gentleness, consistency, and trust. He has no labels for these traits, but he knows how they feel. Giving your child a "feel" for these Christian virtues should be your goal during the first year.

One of your most powerful tools during your child's infancy is music. Sing all day to your baby. Go for a walk and sing to him about the lovely things Jesus has made: butterflies, trees, flowers, birds. Sing about how much Jesus loves him and about how much you love Jesus. Songs communicate to babies in ways that words alone can't.

A young mother lay on her bed suffering from the flu. She felt reasonably good while remaining on her back; but the moment she sat up, waves of intense nausea hit her. To make a bad situation worse, her husband was out of town, and she had a six-month-old daughter to care for. The child sat at her side for a short time but soon became restless, wanting some attention.

Sing, rather than speak. The mother considered several possible activities for the child and finally realized that all she could do was hold a book in the air and read to her daughter while both of them lay on their backs. Taking an illustrated alphabet book, she tried talking to her child about the book, but the baby was obviously uninterested. Then she hit upon the idea of singing a little song about each page. "Jesus made the apple," she sang; the child perked up. "Who made the good banana?" she continued. Still the child paid close attention. Page after page she sang, all the way from A to Z. At the end of the book, the girl indicated that she wanted to repeat the process. So the two of them went through the entire book again. Afterward the mother always sang Bible verses and stories to her child, rather than just trying to say them.

Where can you learn all these songs about Jesus and His gifts? Like the mother in the story, you make them up as you go

Attend your child's class. along, choosing words appropriate for the child's level of development. You might also accompany your child to the infants' class at church (if your church has one). Here you will hear many songs appropriate for tiny children and you will also gain some new ideas for home worship. Don't overlook the benefits your baby will receive from attending the regular church service. Don't leave him in the nursery every week. It's never too early to begin.

Pray before each baby feeding. You have another means to help lead your tiny baby to Christ—*prayer*. Give a simple prayer of thanks each time you begin to feed him—and during the first year of life, that will be often! One young mother began right in the hospital when she fed her baby for the first time. She put the baby's tiny hands together and thanked Jesus for the good milk he was going to drink. She continued this practice, and before the child was a year old, he folded his own hands and waited for prayer before eating!

Repeat the same prayer. During the first year of life, use the same prayer over and over. It can be something like, "Dear Jesus, thank you for my food. Amen." Children learn best from repetition, especially when they have so few verbal skills. Later, as your child learns to talk, you can begin to thank Jesus for each kind of food. But for now, keep it as simple as possible.

Hold your baby as you pray. What about formal worship for an infant? Some parents begin having worship—complete with songs, Bible stories, and prayer—from the day the child comes home from the hospital. They start filling the child's "memory bank" right from the start. One couple I read about chose to include their newborn baby in their formal home worship. They laid their new daughter on the bed when they knelt for prayer and encircled her with their arms as they talked with God. Other parents have chosen to concentrate on informal worship during the first few months, singing songs and talking to their child about Jesus throughout the day rather than having a specific time or format for worship.

Whatever method you choose, the most important thing is that you *introduce your child to Jesus and His love*. Don't be concerned that he won't understand what you are talking about. Larry Christenson insists that even a nursing child can "know" Jesus intuitively—"Thou didst make me hope when I was upon my mother's breasts" (Ps. 22:9b). Even the tiniest child can receive the love and hope of Christ for himself!

12. Six Months To Two Years

As the child grows, he progresses from being a "sponge" to being a great imitator. He stills soaks in all that he sees, hears, smells, feels, and tastes, but now he learns also to respond. When Mother smiles, he smiles. When Daddy claps his hands, Baby tries to clap. This is an excellent time to begin formal worship.

Of course, you will want to keep worship very simple and short so that it won't be too wearing on baby or parents. Start with a brief prayer, a song with actions for the baby to do and a very brief lesson.

One father, concerned that worship be a positive experience for his youngster, has gone so far as to name it "Happy Time!" The name alone will not insure success, but it is certainly a good beginning.

Prayer

Start with one-sentence prayers. Introduce your baby to prayer gradually just as you have with prayer before meals. Start with one sentence, such as, "Dear Jesus, thank you for Mommy and Daddy. Amen"; or "Dear Jesus, thank you for my Bible storybook. Amen." Speak slowly and distinctly, yet as naturally as possible, so that your baby will know that you are talking to *Someone*. Babies and toddlers are great imitators, so you should kneel, close your eyes, and fold your hands—just like you'll want your child to do later. Fold your little one's hands and hold them between yours during prayer. This will train him as well as give him some of the loving physical contact he needs.

During this eighteen-month span, your child will change a great deal. He will begin to acquire vocabulary; he will learn to crawl, then walk, then run. He will change from a completely dependent baby to a fairly independent child. This is a crucial period for teaching worship habits to your child.

Your child begins with virtually no prayer skills as we know them. He cannot talk, he cannot kneel. He won't learn these behaviors overnight, either. He may say a few words at fourteen months, but that doesn't mean he will say them during prayer. He may also have the physical ability to kneel, but will probably refuse to do so. This was the case with my daughter. No amount of coaxing, begging, or even ignoring the situation, would move her to kneel for prayer. She simple refused to do it. About the time I decided that she would *never* kneel, and all my efforts had been in vain, she decided to cooperate.

Many parents have similar experiences. The desired behaviors will emerge "full blown" just about the time parents decide that their child will never acquire them. The child will one day join in "singing" a song, doing all the appropriate actions—but Mom and Dad may have been setting the example for months to no apparent avail. Force is not appropriate here, but rather, kind, patient persistence, with a trust that the child who sees a joyous and reverent attitude toward God will himself learn the pleasure of worship.

Increase complexity of your prayers. Just because your child shows no apparent progress in prayer doesn't mean you should avoid making your prayers more advanced. Don't continue those one-sentence prayers for the full eighteen months. Gradually enlarge the original prayer, both in content and length. Ask Jesus to be present with you, then thank Him that He has come. Thank Jesus for whatever your child especially likes—a certain person, an animal or a toy. Make your prayers as relevant to the child as possible. As he grows older, ask Jesus to forgive your child for disobeying, then ask Him to help the child to obey in the future. (Be sure to do this in love, not with a critical attitude.)

Use "fill-in-the-blank" prayers. Eventually your child will be able to say a few words in prayer by himself, but he will need much help from you. I have found that "fill in the blank" praying helps with my daughter. I begin, "Dear Jesus, thank you for Mommy. Thank you also for _____." (She will usually say, "Daddy.") Encourage your child by repeating anything he says on his own. If he says, "Daddy," in the above example, you can repeat, "Yes, thank you for Daddy." This tells your child that what he said was important to you and to Jesus.

Songs

Sing action songs. Even before children learn to talk, they love to hear songs and participate in them if possible. Therefore, concentrate on songs that have some type of action the child can do: clapping, pointing, swaying, nodding, hopping (with your help). Sing these to your child during worship and always do the accompanying actions.

What we said about prayer applies here, too. Your child may watch you day after day, even month after month, and make no apparent effort to imitate. You may begin to ask, "What's the use?" Then one day, without being prompted, your child will join in the song and do all the actions, loving every minute of it. This will make all the effort worthwhile!

Little children especially enjoy simple rhythm instruments such as bells or rattles. Get enough instruments so that the entire family can join in.

Encourage any kind of participation of which your child is capable. In a short time, he will, almost miraculously, grow from a baby who sits on the sidelines of family singing to a toddler who marches around the house singing his favorite song—and singing well enough for you to recognize the song!

Bible Story

A six-month-old child won't understand much about a Bible story, but a two-year-old will understand a great deal. Somewhere between these two ages your child will begin to grasp what you are telling him. Since we can't predict with certainty when this occurs, we must answer a very practical question: Is it better to start a child too early on Bible lessons or is it more profitable to wait, even if it means we risk waiting too long?

In light of Psalm 22:9 ("But thou art he that took me out of the womb: thou didst make me hope when I was upon my mother's breasts"), it seems we should start early and take advantage of every opportunity to tell our child about Jesus.

Use simple, uncluttered pictures. Of course, these first Bible lessons will be very simple and very explicit. This is definitely the age for visual aids, and lots of them. Buy or make several books to illustrate principles of God's love for us—books with large, simple pictures or drawings. Small children cannot discern fine visual details. Therefore use pictures that are as uncluttered as possible, preferably with one figure per page.

A child's main frame of reference is his family—his mother, his father, his brothers and sisters. Therefore, begin with the topic of the family. Show your child the most beautiful picture of Jesus you can find. Tell him that this is Jesus, and that Jesus loves him very much. Next show your child a picture of Mommy. Tell him, "Jesus loves you so much He gave you a Mommy." Continue with the other family members if your child seems interested. Use this same theme day after day, for young children thrive on repetition.

Use familiar concepts. Perhaps the next thing your child knows best is a pet. Hold your child as he pets the animal and again tell him, "Jesus loves you so much that He gave you a puppy." Continue branching out to things your child is familiar with: food, animals, friends (yours and his), and anything else that he is learning about.

A variety of visual aids will help keep your child as interested as possible. Beside pictures, you can use real objects (whenever possible). When you tell your child about the good fruit that

Jesus provides, bring out real bananas, apples,
Use tangible and grapes to illustrate your point. Your child
objects, if will love to handle them while you talk to him of
possible. Jesus' love. Stuffed animals or even real animals
(puppies, lambs, kittens, rabbits, etc.) are a special treat. Be sure that the stuffed animals are as lifelike as possible so that you won't confuse your child.

Felts are another great asset. You can make your own or buy them at a local Christian bookstore. When my daughter was almost a year old, I made a simple felt set to illustrate Creation. I already had a beautiful felt of Jesus. (This is something you will almost certainly want to buy because you want your child to love and revere Jesus. It is hard to design such a felt, especially if your artistic talents are like mine!) I put the felt of Jesus on one side of a small felt board (I used the inside of the box my baby book came in, covering it with a square of navy blue felt.), and on the other side I put up, one at a time, different things Jesus created—a yellow sun, an orange moon, white stars. These were obviously very simple and required almost no time to make. But my daughter loved the presentation so much that she would go to the bookcase where I kept the felts, reach up, and beg for "worpee." Allow your child to put the different objects on the felt board; this will increase his interest in and enthusiasm for worship.

Make "animal boxes" for your child. Cover a
Make box with bright wrappings (a solid color is best)
"animal and then glue a picture of an animal to the top of
boxes." the box. As near to the animal's mouth as possible, cut a hole in the box top through which your child can "feed" the animal. Purchase plastic worms at a sporting goods store to feed a bird—children love them! Use real peanuts to feed an elephant, or imitation berries (from a florist or craft shop) to feed a bear. Cows can be fed artificial greenery you've cut into small pieces. With these boxes you can introduce your child to all the wonderful animals that God made and tell him that Jesus provides food for each of them.

When your child is a little older, buy some felts (or cut out some pictures and back them with felt) of a modern family, everyday objects and animals your child is familiar with. Use these to teach practical lessons on obedience, sharing, helping others, etc.

Substitute animals for people. For a lesson on obedience, you could put a mother on one side of the felt board and a small child on the other. Say, "When Mother calls, you come running." Then make the little child "run" across the felt board to Mother. Do this several times and then let your child make the felt child "run." If during the day you call and your child doesn't respond, remind him of the worship lesson. This will help apply the lesson to his daily life. Reinforce this idea of obedience by using animal felts. Ask, "When Mother Rabbit calls, who comes running?" Your child will delight to see the little bunny "hop" to his mother. This can be more effective than using people!

Instill *positive* ideas. Whatever behavior you are trying to instill in your child, you can do it with pictures. But always show him the *right* behavior, never the wrong one. Fill his mind with good, positive thoughts.

As your child approaches two years of age, he will be able to follow a simple story. Therefore, get some Bible picture books and a set of Bible felts at this time. You will need to repeat the same story for at least a week in order that your child may become thoroughly familiar with it. You will also want to alternate between picture books and felts to keep your child's interest high.

As you begin a Bible story, first introduce your child to the characters—"This is Baby Jesus, this is Mary, this is Joseph." Point to the characters as you talk about them. Otherwise, what you say may be confusing or even meaningless to your child.

Avoid unnecessary details. As you tell the story, keep it as simple as possible. Before you describe any aspect of the narrative, ask yourself, Is this necessary? Will my child understand the story if I leave this out? The simpler the story, the more likely your child is to understand its message. If you're telling about Elijah and the Brook Cherith, you don't need to explain why he fled there. Begin by telling your child where Elijah was and that he was hungry. There will be plenty of time later to add the details.

Above all, tell the Bible story with enthusiasm. Make your child "see" what happened by the way you tell the story. Keep the narrative moving; don't drag it out and lose your child's interest.

Your child can participate in the Bible story even before he is able to talk. After he becomes familiar with the various characters in the story, let him point them out to you. Ask him, "Where is Elijah?" "Where is the bird that fed Elijah?" "Where is the Brook Cherith?" This will give him the opportunity to reveal how much he understands and, more importantly, will make him feel a part of the worship experience.

Memory Verse

Use a one-word "memory verse."

If you start the "memory verse habit" at this age, you will, of course, have to adapt it to your child's verbal abilities. You might have your child say "Jesus," "God," "angel," or the name of the central character in your Bible story for his memory verse. If he can say simple sentences, you might use "God is love," or some other very basic Bible text.

Content

As was true of the tiny infant, even the two-year-old child needs experiential knowledge that God loves him and that his greatest purpose, in turn, is to love and glorify God. However, whereas infants can relate only to the love of the members of their immediate family, a toddler begins to develop an interest in the world outside his home. He is fascinated by animals—especially dogs—and insects. He delights in watching an ant carry his heavy load or a butterfly floating through the air. As his interests broaden, you should broaden his knowledge of God's love. Reveal God's love to him through a soft white kitten, a bright yellow flower, or a singing red bird. Explain that all good things, all the things we enjoy every day, are given to us by our Lord.

Encourage expressions of love to God.

Encourage expressions of love for Jesus. When he first learns to talk, you might ask, "Whom do you love? Mommy? (Yes.) Daddy? (Yes.) Jesus? (Yes.) Yes, we love Jesus best of all! Teach him, also, to thank Jesus for all the lovely things He has provided: parents, siblings, good food, animals. In prayer before meals, thank Jesus for the specific foods: "Dear Jesus, thank you for my oatmeal, banana, and juice. Amen." This will make prayer more like talking to Jesus and less like a ritual.

13. Two Through Three Years

A chief characteristic of this age group is short attention span. No matter how interesting your worship time, you must keep it short and to the point for a two- or three-year-old child. Have a brief, specific prayer, tell a Bible story in the most interesting manner possible, sing a song or two, have your child repeat his memory verse and reward him with a sticker. Keep things moving with no time for the child to become bored or distracted.

Prayer

Use one- or two- sentence prayers. During prayer time, encourage your child to pray a sentence or two in his own words, perhaps "Dear Jesus, thank you for Mommy and Daddy." Let him choose what to say and encourage him to make it as natural as possible—no thee's and thou's. Don't be surprised at what he comes out with. One night my daughter thanked Jesus that our neighbor's child fell down and cut her head. I tried to reword her prayer with, "Thank you that you will make her head well," or "Thank you she did not get hurt worse." But she persisted in her original prayer. Soon a verse of Scripture came to my mind: "Giving thanks always for *all* things unto God. . . (Eph. 5:20). From then on I let her prayers stand as she said them.

Pray in concrete terms. This is not the time to pray for "bringing salvation to all the world" or even "filling our hearts with your Spirit of truth." Children think in *concrete* terms, and our prayers with them should correspond with their ability to understand them. A two- or three-year-old child will understand "Help me to come quickly when Mommy and Daddy call" far more readily than "Help me to be obedient."

A reminder about prayers with very small children: keep them short. These youngsters tire easily and become restless very quickly. Make your prayer time with them personal, interesting, and brief so that it will be a pleasant experience for them.

Songs

Two- and three-year-old children are just learning to sing, and they love action songs. If you know a song which relates to your Bible story (e.g., "Zacchaeus Was a Wee Little Man," "The Wise Man Built His House Upon a Rock," "Only a Boy Named David"), by all means use it. If not, sing a simple song that is appropriate to the message you are conveying (e.g.,"Jesus Loves Me" or "Oh, How I Love Jesus"). Use rhythm instruments and songs that involve a lot of clapping and other body movements.

Bible Story

"Save" the miracle stories. Two- and three-year-old children are becoming newly acquainted with the many exciting stories of the Bible. They hear about Adam and Eve, David, Moses, Noah, and even God, for the first time. They have no preconceptions or prejudices with which to color their interpretation of the Bible stories. Nothing is too incredible, too unusual, too amazing for them to believe. They have not yet discovered the rules of logic which temper our day-to-day existence; they look upon even the most amazing miracles of the Bible as if they were everyday occurrences. For this reason, you may want to avoid the miracle stories when you relate Bible stories to your child of this age. If you tell him about Jesus' feeding the five thousand, he will most likely see nothing noteworthy in His action. How much better to wait until he has learned what to expect in day-to-day life; then he can thrill to the wonderful way that Jesus can miraculously care for His children.

Continue to use visual aids in relating Bible stories, but now you can use picture books and church magazines or papers with illustrated stories. Children of this age love to "read" stories by telling what they see in each picture. They learn to do this by watching the pictures as you tell the Bible story.

Allow the child to retell the story.
Since children of two and three thrive on repetition, you can tell or read the same story every day for a week, perhaps emphasizing a different aspect of the story each day. After your child has learned the story, have him tell you the story one day for worship. This will help keep him involved and will also indicate how well he understands what you have been telling him.

It is vital that *you* believe a story before you try to make it believable to your child. Your tone of voice and your attitude toward the story is just as important as the words you say. Consider again the story of Elijah, this time from the perspective of a two- or three-year-old. Try to imagine how you would relate this story if you had been an eyewitness. Almost certainly you would not parrot the usual, "Elijah was hungry and some birds brought him food." Perhaps you would describe how far he was from any supply of food, how he dared not leave the Brook Cherith (where God told him to stay) in order to look for food, how his situation seemed hopeless without divine intervention. Tell how tired and lonely Elijah felt and how he longed for some sign of God's presence. Tell of his curiosity, his wonderment, and even possible fright as huge ravens flew closer and closer, heading straight for him. It must have taken Elijah some time to recognize that these birds were bringing food. Imagine his amazement when they flew right to him and dropped food into his hand. Could there be a more direct answer to prayer?

Speak as if you see the events unfolding before your eyes; let your voice reveal excitement, suspense or sorrow; even act out appropriate parts to the story. Use anything else—sound effects, costumes, etc.—to make it more vivid to the listener.

For young children it is also helpful to have them repeat key words or concepts as the story progresses. In our story of Elijah, the child could repeat "Elijah," "Brook Cherith," "raven," and

Use fill-in-
the-blank
stories.

"food." As the child becomes more familiar with the story, have him "fill in the blank." You can say, "This is a story about _____ (child says, "Elijah") as you put up a picture or felt of Elijah. Then you may say, "God told Elijah to go to the _____ ("Brook Cherith"). This helps the child in two ways: It keeps him involved and interested in the worship because he knows that he will be called upon frequently. It also helps cement the names and concepts of the story in his mind.

As your child approaches his third birthday, begin to ask him a few questions about the Bible story after you've finished telling it (providing he isn't getting too restless). If you told the story of Rebekah giving water to the camels, you could ask, "Why did Rebekah give water to the thirsty camels?" (She was kind); "What can *you* do that is kind?" (Share my toys with Baby Brother); "How can you be kind to Daddy?" (Rub his feet when he is tired); "How can you be kind to Mommy?" (Pick up my toys). This will stimulate your child's thinking and will help him relate the Bible story to his personal life, showing him that the Bible is given not for information or entertainment but to show us God's plan for our lives.

Try supplementing Bible stories with devotional books designed for young children. *Today I Feel Like a Warm Fuzzy** and *Today I Feel Loved**, both by William L. Coleman, help children to gain a biblical understanding of their own emotions.

Memory Verse

Two- and three-year-old children are rapidly developing verbal skills, so now is a good time to begin teaching them Bible verses. They will memorize frequently repeated verses of Scripture almost as soon as they learn to talk. Don't underestimate their ability! It may take some creativity on your part to get your child to say their Bible verse, but what a thrill to hear him repeating God's Word!

I remember in particular one worship experience I had with a three-year-old, a two-and-a-half-year-old, and a child not yet

*Bethany House Publishers.

two. The two older children easily recited, "I always do what is pleasing to Him." Then I had the youngest child say "Jesus" for her memory verse. Before closing the worship session I wanted to reinforce the verse in the memory of the older children, so I said, "I always (pause)," and waited for them to fill in the missing word. The older children were distracted with something else, but the youngest said, "Do."

I could hardly believe my ears, for she could barely say a few words. So I tried again. "I always _____." She again said, "Do." I went on, "what is pleasing to _____." She said, "Him."

When I told the child's mother about my experience, she was as amazed as I was, but also encouraged to begin teaching the child a memory verse weekly.

Rewards

A well-chosen reward for saying the memory verse might easily make the difference between a child's casual acceptance of family worship and his eager anticipation of it. We all like to receive a little "bonus" for a job well done, and children seem especially appreciative of such little rewards in life.

Reward memorization with stickers. When she was about two years old, I began giving my daughter a gummed star each day she said her memory verse. When her friends came over and we all had worship together, they were just as eager as she to choose a star and stick it somewhere, anywhere. Sometimes they put stars on the lesson booklet, sometimes on their stomachs! The first question they asked when I announced, "It's time for worship," was, "Do we get a sticker?"

Because stars proved so much fun, we tried "nature stickers": dogs, cats, birds, butterflies, flowers, wild animals. We tried to get stickers that were related to Jesus and the things He created. Later on we used stickers of angels, Bibles, etc.

Be sure to store your stickers in an inaccessible place—children love them so much they almost can't resist getting a few extra when you're not having worship.

Problems

Tell a Bible story as a special secret. What do you do if you've followed all these suggestions and your two- or three-year-old occasionally still balks at family worship? Don't be discouraged. Children of this age tire easily, and when they're tired, nothing goes right! Maybe this would be a good time to hold the child in your lap, sing a few quiet songs, and softly tell him the Bible story as if it were a special secret, just between you and him.

Maybe your child just won't settle down long enough to hear a story; maybe he loves to stay on the go. Then try playing "church" with him. Everybody can pretend to drive in the car to church, get out and go to class, sing a few lively songs, then hopefully sit still long enough to hear a brief story. Act out the story with your child (include props, too). He will love the attention and, with God's help, will learn to love the Bible at the same time.

Content

Your first Bible stories for the child of two or three should concentrate on God's love. Tell your child about how God took care of Daniel in the lions' den and about how God used birds to feed Elijah. Tell him in more detail about God making a beautiful world for us because He loves us. Tell how God loved Hannah and Elkanah so much that He gave them a special baby. In the New Testament, you will find lots of stories that tell of Jesus' love for us. Children especially like the story of Zacchaeus.

Many of the stories of Jesus' miracles can be used, too, if we emphasize the love rather than miracle. When you tell about Jesus feeding the multitude, emphasize how hungry the people were and how Jesus wanted to give them good food. Above all, your child should learn that God loves him and that Jesus is his Friend. Use stories that illustrate these truths and tell the stories in such a way that these truths are the central message.

The teaching of discipline continues to be one of your chief tasks at this age, so you will want to tell Bible stories that encourage obedience. The story of Adam and Eve's disobedience and subsequent punishment will help the child understand that he too must be punished when he disobeys, even though (and because) you love him very much. You will also want to illustrate obedience and its rewards. Consider the story of the disciples' fishing all night without results—not even one fish. In the morning Jesus told them to try one more time, throwing the net on the right side of the boat. They obeyed because they loved Jesus (not because it seemed the sensible thing to do) and were rewarded by the largest catch of fish they had ever pulled in.

To encourage a thankful heart in your child, tell him how the biblical characters appreciated God's love. You can be sure that Daniel was thankful for the angel who protected him, that the people in the hungry multitude were glad they didn't have to make their way back home with empty stomachs, that Zacchaeus was grateful for a friend.

14. Four Through Five Years

Children in this age group are a seeming paradox. On the one hand, they have matured and gained increased understanding and self-control. They are more cooperative, have a greater intellectual grasp of biblical truths, and have a much longer attention span than before. On the other hand, they have abundant energy and need much activity. How does one incorporate these characteristics into the family worship setting?

Prayer

Encourage prayer about everything.

Four- and five-year-olds are learning to express themselves well verbally, and they love to practice this newly-developed skill. They like to talk, talk, talk! You can put this desire to use in worship by encouraging your child to take an active part in family prayer. He will be able to say several sentences—preferably not the same ones over and over each day. Help him talk to Jesus about the events, people, and surroundings of his daily life—the things that are of immediate interest to him. Help him to realize that he can talk to Jesus about *everything*—the quarrel with Johnny, the neighbor who is in the hospital, the new toy he wants for his birthday.

Remember that children of his age have tremendous faith; they trust completely if experience has not taught them otherwise. These characteristics put them especially close to God. Be very careful not to damage this precious faith. Nurture it, for all too soon your little one will encounter doubts and ridicule as he ventures out into the world beyond his immediate family.

If your child seems reluctant to participate in family prayer, continue very gently to encourage him. This is an age when the child is especially receptive to the leading of the Holy Spirit. He has passed from the unreasoned impulsiveness and emotionality of toddlerhood, but has not yet come into extensive contact with an unchristian world. Make the most of every opportunity to point him to Jesus. Help him to develop his childlike faith. Teach him to know Jesus as his best Friend.

Songs

Because of his abundant energy at this age, it is still a good idea to use many action songs, although you will want them to be more advanced than those for the earlier age groups. You should also begin teaching your child a few hymns; he can march to "Onward Christian Soldiers," and pretend blowing a horn (or play a real one) to "Lift Up the Trumpet." He also might enjoy songs that involve interaction—you sing a question and the child sings the answer—such as "When a Mother Says Bow-wow, Who Comes Running?" or "Oh, Mary, Do You Love Jesus?" The most important thing, however, as with all worship, is that the child enjoys singing with you. Make it as pleasant (even fun) as possible.

Bible Story

Reinforce stories with field trips.

Four- and five-year-olds obviously have a greater intellectual capacity than younger children. They are very curious and want to experience everything through their senses, especially the sense of touch. This is a good time to step up your use of visual aids. Let your child help you think of appropriate "props" to make a story more meaningful. For instance, if you're studying about the disciples fishing on the Sea of Galilee, go to a sporting goods store and let your child see and feel a real fishing net. Take him to a nearby river and let him see how people fish today.

Children of this age also have a great deal of energy, so encourage yours to act out the Bible stories after he has become acquainted with them. Let him "direct" the production: gather props, choose each person's role, etc. This will channel his energy and get him heavily involved in the worship experience. Perhaps he could even paint or color scenery on large sheets of paper.

Four- and five-year-olds need to begin practicing Bible truths in earnest. They need to learn that the Bible is not just a collection of fascinating stories but rather is a guidebook for Christian living. They can make up skits depicting biblical principles such as obedience, sharing, and self-sacrifice.

Discuss relationship problems. By all means, encourage your child to put these principles into action in real life as well. Discuss with him the problems he has with interpersonal relationships ("Billy always picks on me."), family jealousies ("You love the baby more than me."), and fears ("I don't want you to turn all the lights out."). Give him Bible answers to the questions of everyday life. Point him to the life of Jesus and show how Jesus coped with all the problems of life, big and small.

Develop "others-consciousness." Begin to develop "others-consciousness" in your child. If he has a friend who is ill, help your child make up for the friend a basket filled with things children like: books, apples, wild flowers, a puzzle. If you are trying to teach your child to share, encourage him to gather up some of his clothing and toys to give to the poor. Of course, remember that your child will learn more from watching how *you* relate to a friend's illness or poverty than he will get from a hundred verbal lessons.

Tell Bible stories from various viewpoints. As you teach your child Bible stories, it is still a good idea to repeat them frequently. Children of this age forget easily and need repetition to make the story or lesson "stick." Prevent your child from becoming bored by varying the story each day. If you're telling the story of Jonah, for instance, tell it once as a narrative, once from Jonah's viewpoint, once from God's viewpoint, and once from the viewpoint of a sailor on board the ship; then let your child tell the story for several days.

Memory Verse

Four- and five-year-olds have a great capacity for memorization. They memorize everything they hear, from children's storybooks to television commercials. Why not harness this special ability at the time when it is so strong? Let your child stockpile large portions of Scripture now; later, when memorization of Scripture will become more difficult, he will be able to retrieve previously learned verses with ease.

A few years ago I taught the kindergarten class at our church—four-, five-, and six-year-olds. One quarter we had a special memorization project: each child who could say twelve Bible verses (with no prompting except a picture illustrating the appropriate verse) would receive a package from our treasure chest. Each week for twelve weeks we went over the Bible verses: the first week one verse, the fifth week five verses, the twelfth week twelve verses. On the thirteenth week, each child would have an opportunity to demonstrate what he had learned. One after another these little children came to the front of the room and recited twelve different Bible verses. I was thrilled that their minds were being filled with God's Word.

Add mystery to memory motivators. Don't underestimate your child's ability. Challenge him to learn God's Word for himself. Then offer him an appropriate reward—a Bible storybook, an afternoon alone with you, even his first real Bible with his name imprinted on it. Add a little mystery to the reward. Wrap the Bible storybook or Bible with beautiful paper and a bow. Don't tell him exactly what it is. (He'll probably guess it's a book of some kind, but that's all right.) If you're going to spend a special afternoon with him, tell him so, but don't tell him what the two of you will be doing. Not only will he be motivated to earn his reward, but perhaps, even more, he will be intrigued by its hidden details. This sort of motivator will be much more effective with this age group than will stickers. The child is expending more effort to learn many memory verses instead of just one, and he will appreciate a special reward for his labors.

Content

Several years ago Swiss psychologist Jean Piaget observed and recorded the various stages of learning through which children progress as they mature intellectually; he found that the four- and five-year-old's learning tasks center around discovering the rules which govern his world. The child learns that life is, to a large extent, predictable, and he strives to understand those laws which make it so.

Teach the Ten Commandments. This is an ideal time, therefore, to teach your child God's rules for living, the Ten Commandments. Introduce the commandments by talking to your child about his favorite game, maybe hide and seek. Discuss with him the rules of this game and why they are important. Maybe a toddler has tried to join in his game recently and spoiled the whole thing by going around and pointing out hiding places. This will help the child understand why we need rules to live by and why we need to obey them. Help him to understand that God gives us rules because He loves us and wants us to be happy.

Tell your child some of the reasoning behind God's rules, but don't get discouraged if he finds this discussion somewhat irrelevant. Children of this age tend to be "legalists"—they see laws as more important than the people to whom the laws are given. They operate under a system of absolute morality where laws are fixed and rigid.

Introduce the plan of salvation. The content of your worship should center, now and at every age, on God's love. This is as true when teaching the child about God's principles as when telling him about the plan of salvation, a subject you might want to introduce now.

Use devotional books. Start adding to your worship format short stories which teach biblical lessons. Some families use this type of story to set the mood of togetherness and reverence before they begin their formal worship. Children of four and five love stories—beg for them, in fact—so this will add one more bonus to help them look forward to worship. Devotional books for

98

young children are a great asset for this activity. *Singing Penguins and Puffed-Up Toads* and *Counting Stars*, both by William Coleman, are fascinating devotional books for this age group.*

A Quiet Time

In spite of a child's need for activity, he also can learn to appreciate quietness at this age. A quiet spirit, and even silence in our bustling world, is a rare commodity nowadays, but we can give this priceless gift to our children if we are willing to develop it ourselves.

Find a peaceful environment. Anna Mow writes about a family with several small children who had just spent a long, tiring day sight-seeing. They stopped at some picnic tables beside the highway to eat their supper; but the excitement of the day plus the constant noise and motion of passing cars made it virtually impossible for the children to settle down properly. The mother wisely began packing up the supper, suggesting that they find a more secluded spot. Finally they discovered a spot beside a small stream away from the confusion of the highway. Each family member seemed to relax almost at once, absorbing the peacefulness of the water and trees. The child who had been the most active and the least able to calm down spoke for all of them when he said, "This is just what I wanted." He realized and appreciated the intrinsic value of quietness only after he had experienced it.

"Play quiet." All children need quiet times to rest and sort out their thoughts, experiences, and desires; but how do we get them to settle down long enough to experience quietness? One method of teaching our children to value silence and physical rest is by "playing quiet" with them. Whispering, "Let's see how long we can be quiet together," certainly is more effective than yelling, "Will you sit down and be quiet!" Of course, beginning to have worship with an infant will have initiated him somewhat in the value of silence and spiritual meditation.

---

*Bethany House Publishers.

Consider setting aside a special time each day that you and your child (or children) can spend in silence. Read a book while your child looks at books or plays with puzzles. The two of you might try lying in bed a few minutes even if your child no longer takes a nap.

15. Six Through Nine Years

In their years from six through nine, children's lives broaden in scope. Most of them enter school during this age range; they face strong peer pressure and greater personal responsibility. Furthermore, during this stage, children's special talents begin to appear and thus need to be developed. But discovering where one's talents lie can be a real challenge, especially when one is so young. We should therefore focus during home worship on helping our children find their unique gifts with which to serve the Lord.

The format for worship remains much the same from this age on; you will nearly always have prayer, a lesson from the Bible, and perhaps some singing. But within this basic framework, there is room for tremendous variety and creativity.

Prayer

Children of this age group still live very much in the present. They will be more likely to pray for help on today's test than for a home with Jesus for eternity. Encourage your child to pray about every detail of his life, to bring every joy and every problem to his Heavenly Friend. Talk much with your child so that you can guide him in his prayer life.

Teach the Lord's Prayer. This would be a good age to teach your child the Lord's Prayer. Pray it together every night for a week until your child becomes familiar with it. During the following week study the prayer in depth as your Bible lesson. During the third week have your child memorize the Lord's Prayer. This will teach your child about the many aspects of prayer: praising God, submitting to Him, acknowledging His authority, asking for needs, requesting forgiveness, yielding our lives to Him. This will help your child progress beyond the usual "Thank you for. . . . Bless Mommy, Daddy. . . . Help me to be good " prayer.

Songs

Let your child teach new songs. You can help your child develop his musical talents. If he has a gift for singing or playing a musical instrument, let him provide "special music" one day a week. The rest of the time you can let him lead out in family singing or accompany singing on the piano, trumpet, etc. He will probably be learning many new songs at church and school, so let him teach these to the rest of the family.

Bible Study

The study of the Bible will afford you many opportunities to discover and develop your child's abilities. Since at this age he is learning to read, he can now more actively participate in the lesson. Allow him to read a portion of the Scripture each day or maybe the entire Scripture one day a week. In either case, you let him know beforehand what he will read so that he can practice. This will accomplish two goals: First, by asking him to *prepare* for Bible reading, you show that worship is important—not something to stumble through. Second, your child will become much more familiar with the Bible by reading it over and over by himself than he would by hearing you read it once.

If your child is just learning to read, help him prepare before worship—this will provide you an opportunity to give the focused attention (eye contact and physical contact also) that tells your child how much you love him. If you find that your child excels in reading aloud, encourage him to develop this ability. Take him to the library or bookstore and let him choose a special book he would like to read during worship. Perhaps he could read a page every day. Let this be something just for worship—if he reads part of it any other time, the rest of the family will miss out. (Devotional books such as *My Magnificent Machine** would be excellent for this.)

Draw or color to illustrate the story. Does your child have a talent for drawing or painting? You can encourage this ability by having him create a picture depicting the Bible lesson for the day. If your budding artist is the youngest member of the family, let him draw while the rest of the family discusses the lesson in depth. This will keep him from becoming bored or restless and will promote his participation. It will also motivate him to listen more closely to the lesson so he can know which details to draw. You might want to tell your child about well-known artists who have devoted their talents to God, such as Harry Anderson and Joni Eareckson. Even if your child is not artistically talented, encourage him to draw his impressions of the story, or to color a related picture in a Bible coloring book.

Allow child to write stories in his own words. If your child likes to write, have him write Bible stores in his own words. And if he is especially creative, he might like to write modern-day stories which teach the same lessons you are studying in the Bible. These can be read to the whole family at worship, but only if it doesn't make the child self-conscious. Take your would-be writer to the library, too, and let him know that all writers started out just like he is doing. Tell him about the different Bible writers—their varied backgrounds and writing styles. Of course, encourage him to pursue his writing for the glory of God.

Play Bible games.** Children of six through nine love games, so adapt some of their favorite games to fit the worship setting. I have found that Bible tic-tac-toe is a great motivator. After reading and discussing a Bible lesson, divide family members into two groups, X's

*Bethany House Publishers.
**An excellent game for building Bible knowledge in people of all ages is *The Amen Game* (Bethany House Publishers, 1981).

and O's. (If there are only three persons, for example, you will have one X, and one O, and one moderator.) The moderator will read a question about the Bible lesson and let the X group try to answer it. If they can't, the O group will have a turn. The next question goes first to the O group. Each group puts either an X or an O on the tic-tac-toe board for every correct answer. The game is scored like regular tic-tac-toe. Make the questions difficult enough to challenge your child's thinking but not so difficult that he cannot answer them.

Occasionally play charades. Let one family member act out a scene from the Bible while everyone else tries to guess what he is portraying. Use an appropriate level of difficulty so that your child will become neither bored nor discouraged. I played charades once with my niece when she was six, and now she asks to play it again almost every time I see her.

Memory Verse

Have family Scripture memorization projects. As you work to fill your child's mind with God's Word by memorization of Bible passages, make memorization a family project. Start with a short psalm, perhaps Psalm 23. Read it in unison every night for a week, or even a month, depending on how long it takes you to learn it. For the first week, study the psalm together in depth in order to understand it more fully. Perhaps you can read it from several different versions. (This can be confusing for memorization, however.) Later make this reading the beginning or end of your worship, and study other Bible passages. Don't become discouraged if it takes you as long as a month to learn a psalm. If you pursue memorization faithfully, at the end of a year you will know twelve psalms (or other Bible passages)!

Should you continue to reward your child for Bible memorization? Should you give him prizes for successfully learning Scripture or should he do this because he wants to, or even because you expect it of him? This is a complex issue and one which you as a parent should decide for yourself. Certainly you cannot continue to give stickers to a child in this age group, so what *can* you do?

Many schools have adopted a system of behavior modification in which students receive a reward for a job well done. The rewards vary from verbal praise to a lunch at the local fast-food restaurant. At times this method seems to have worked well, especially for students who have motivational problems. But it has its limitations, chief of which is the emphasis it puts on *external* motivators. By emphasizing external rewards, you may actually weaken internal motivation. Thus, your child may cease the desired activity when the rewards are removed. This is not to say that you should never use external rewards, because that would be unrealistic. After all, we adults work for external reinforcement: a paycheck at the end of the month, a new outfit when the diet is over. Even the final reward for the Christian—heaven—is in part a tangible, external prize.

The main point is that we don't want to use external rewards exclusively. Use them, but sparingly. Whenever possible try to encourage the internal rewards: the satisfaction of living up to a standard, the knowledge of a job well done, and the joy of learning. Help your child love God's Word by first showing him that *you* love it and want to commit portions of it to memory. And when the time comes that he needs a little extra push, choose the reward wisely. Maybe you could attend a special Christian youth rally with your child. Maybe he has wanted to have a certain record of gospel music; you could buy that for him. As much as possible make the reward an opportunity for further spiritual growth. And, of course, be sure that the reward fits your child. Talk with him about what he would like to have or do, and make that the reward.

Content

Between the ages of six and ten, children must confront a problem which all but tiny infants experience: we as humans by and large know how we should behave, but we have trouble living up to this knowledge. We know that we should tell the truth, but little "white" lies slip out so easily. We know that we should be loving and kind, but tempers flare before we can stop them. We know that we should forgive others, but often we carry a grudge or hurt for months, even years.

A child has the intellectual capacity to begin to grasp the great alienation between Christ and Satan. Explain to him that their two kingdoms desire a person's allegiance. He will better understand the conflicting feelings he has as he debates in his mind between good and evil. Familiar Bible stories will take on new meaning as you point out to him the working of Satan versus the Trinity. Let your child interpret some of his favorite Bible stories in this light.

Once the child realizes that he isn't warring against himself—that he is battling "against principalities, against powers, against the rulers of the darkness of this world, against spiritual wickedness in high places" (Eph. 6:12), he will face another dilemma; he doesn't stand a chance! Now the power of God, Christ, and the Holy Spirit can take on new meaning for him. He can understand that God has infinite resources to help him, that Jesus can empower him to make correct choices and then carry them out. He can accept Christ as his personal Savior and be filled with the Holy Spirit.

Encourage your child to witness. An understanding of his own condition will help make your child more aware of the needs of others. Give him opportunities for outreach to others. Encourage him to visit sick friends, new children in the neighborhood, or the child who's treated like an outcast. Let him invite non-Christian friends to family worship or to church services.

Children of this age have spiritually "turned the corner," so to speak. They begin to develop a "morality of conscience"; they now internalize principles and values rather than relying on external controls (parents). They begin to understand the spirit of the law as well as the letter. It is a crucial time in their spiritual development.

Other Ideas

Two more characteristics of this age group stand out. First of all, these children require calmness and order in their personal lives, perhaps because their social lives are changing so rapidly. They continue to need a quiet time each day to sort out their thoughts, hopes, aspirations, and fears. They also need family strength to lean on when all else seems uncertain. School, with all its new experiences, is a big adjustment for them—the first big step toward independence. We need to be as reassuring, supportive, and stable as possible during this time.

Secondly, children of this age group are still in what is known as the "concrete operational state." They feel more at home with physical objects than with abstract ideas. The time for debating moral issues is still a few years off. Therefore, continue to give them object lessons of Christ's love using things they can physically manipulate. Give your child a mirror and while he is looking at himself, put some catsup or black smudge on his face. Now tell him that the Bible is like a mirror, that helps us to see sin and weakness in our lives. Just as we can wash our faces clean again as we look in the mirror, even so we can let Jesus cleanse us from sin as we study and meditate on His Word and live according to its principles.

Give clues about the next day's lesson. Make Bible study more intriguing for this age group by keeping secret which story or passage will be read next. As you finish one day's study, give clues about the subject of the next day's reading—don't be too obvious. This will keep the children guessing; their minds will be focused on God's Word rather than some less noble topic.

In the same vein, you could tell the beginning of a story on one day—stating a problem, such as "What would Jesus do if. . . ?" Then the next day, ask for each family member's conclusion. This will help keep the topic of worship in their minds between periods of formal worship.

16. Ten Through Twelve Years

Up till this age, your child probably has accepted your beliefs, values, and life-style without much question. The importance of family worship has gone unchallenged. However, the situation may change somewhere between ten and thirteen. Suddenly your ideas on character development and your rules and beliefs to live by may not sit well with your child. He may become aloof in worship, seeming to go into a shell, especially if he has friends that encourage this sort of behavior. What can you do to avoid this problem if it hasn't already arisen, or overcome it if it now confronts you?

The key to spiritual motivation at this age is showing your child his need of God. If Christianity is not relevant to his everyday life, he may well cast it aside or at least give it a minor role in his life. Since all aspects of worship center around this crucial issue, we will forego the separate section on prayer, Bible study, etc., and will instead discuss some general ideas that can be adapted to all phases of worship.

Preteens generally stay on the go. They like to *do* things rather than *talk* about them. They enjoy adventure and discovery. They are likely to be loud, boisterous, and competitive. The peer group wields strong influence during this age.

Justice and fair play are very important to preteens. Unfortunately, these youngsters sometimes feel that their peer group embodies these principles but that their parents (who of necessity must exert some restraint on their children) avoid them.

This is a time, also, of hero worship; naturally, a great discrepancy can exist between the heroes which preteens admire and those which their parents wish they would admire.

These characteristics paint a rather gloomy picture for the parent who wants to maintain a strong influence over his child. They call attention to the growing independence his child is asserting. But this situation also presents parents with the opportunity to help their youngster to think increasingly for himself and yet make decisions of which his parents approve. This is not the time for parents to crack down on their children, but rather to lovingly guide them.

Children must learn to internalize rules and moral guidelines. If a child does as he has been told only out of fear, if he has no personal interest or motivation in growing in Christ, then he will be sorely vulnerable to worldly influences and temptations when he leaves the safety of home and parents. Likewise, he may also face moral corruption if he has not learned precisely what God expects of him and *why*. Many children from "good homes" have gone astray during early adulthood (and, increasingly, during early adolescence) because their parents did not think it necessary to take the time to instruct them "in righteousness."

Concentrate on relevant issues. Bible lessons for older children should concentrate on relevant issues: drugs, sexual mores, dress, etc., with an emphasis—a strong emphasis—on the reasons behind God's laws and prohibitions. "Because I said so," or even "because God says so," is not sufficient explanation for a young person who is seeking to understand the complexities of modern life. Surely a child should be taught to obey God in all things, but wherever possible, explanation of the reasons behind God's laws should be provided. Expecting the child to exercise "blind faith" on all issues is very unwise.

Explain the reasons behind God's laws. Parents must possess two qualifications in order to give truly effective guidance and direction: they must know their child, and they must know their Bible. If you really know your child, his joys, his problems, his strengths and his weaknesses, you will be able to communicate with him effectively during family worship and during the rest of the day as well. You will know what special needs he has, what doubts or questions plague his mind, what insecurities mar his self-esteem. And if you know your Bible, you will be able to give him specific biblical answers to these needs, doubts, and insecurities. You can have worship that is tailor-made to your child, worship that is relevant.

Use a problem-solution format. As you worship together, start right at the heart of the matter—your child's needs. Get his attention early in worship by focusing on some problem—his or someone else's. Human beings seem fascinated by problems—perhaps they give us a sense of kinship with other humans or maybe they challenge us to come up with a solution. Whatever the reason, announcing a problem can "hook" your preteen's interest. Read a newspaper article or a letter from "Dear Ann"; read or make up a short story or parable; set up an imaginary scene: "You meet Judas as he is leaving the temple where he has just betrayed Christ. What would you say to him? How does he feel?"

Whichever method you employ, emphasize a problem that needs to be solved, a question that needs to be answered. Then use the remainder of the prayer and Bible study time to find and discuss solutions.

One adaption of this idea lets each person work out the problem for himself. This should work especially well with the preteen since it allows him some independence of thought—you are not telling him what he ought to think. Propose a problem situation: "Mary goes to a friend's house for a slumber party. When she arrives, she finds that the friend's parents are out of town and that the other girls are drinking. What should she do?"

After every person arrives at his own conclusions, *backed up by Scripture*, the family can discuss the various solutions. Of course, you will want to adapt the problem situation to your children's social and emotional maturity. But don't neglect to confront relevant issues. Even if you don't face them at home, you can be sure that your child will face them in school.

Another variation on this idea is the hypothetical, "If Jesus were here, would he. . . ?" Again, make it relevant. Help your

110

child develop the habit of thinking through life's issues, not just following the crowd. "If Jesus were here, would He . . . (try to make good grades in school or just get by? dress like everyone else? help a friend out in a fight? go to church, even if He found it dull?)." Always use the Bible as the basis of your discussions. Your child needs to know what *God* has to say about the issues of his life.

Begin a story; let your child finish it. You can also try beginning a story and letting your youngster finish it. Some parents have used this painless method to teach children moral lessons when they have erred. The parent tells a story (without mentioning names, of course) about the errant behavior, and then let the child describe what should have been done.

If your child's a gifted writer, challenge him with this task: Take any well-known Bible story and write it from the point of view of one of its characters. If you are studying Christ's feeding the multitude, your preteen can write it from several perspectives: the lad who donated his lunch, one of the disciples, Christ himself, one of the multitude. (Or how about the parents of the young lad? Maybe they accused their son of having an overactive imagination—if not lying—when he told them what had happened.) This might be a good exercise for the whole family, with each family member taking a different viewpoint; it effectively puts *you* into the Bible scene. It is no longer a story which you've heard many times, but an event in which you (through your character) are involved.

Devotional books, such as *Does Anyone Care How I Feel?** by Mildred Tengbom, *Joshua Wiggins and the King's Kids** by Charles Beamer and *On Your Mark** by William L. Coleman deal with issues important to this age group. They are excellent discussion-starters.

*Bethany House Publishers.

17. The Teenage Years—Thirteen Through Nineteen

Adolescence is the most difficult period about which to make psychological generalizations. During roughly seven years, a child becomes an adult, he moves from dependence toward independence and his sexual organs ripen and become functional, greatly increasing his sexual and aggressive drives.

What can be said, then, about a period of life that brings such change, diversity, and even turmoil? How do we gear family devotions to teenage interests? Perhaps the key word here is *internalization.* We want more than ever to encourage a young person to accept biblical principles as his own. We want Christianity to be such a part of him that he will carry it with him wherever he goes—to school, to social gatherings, on dates and at home, as well as to church. We want him to personally experience answered prayer.

But we don't want to use Christianity as a weapon. If we try to enforce our beliefs and values on a teenager without considering his feelings or opinions—if we try to use Scripture to control him externally—we run the risk of embittering him against the Church. Rather, we want to encourage him to exercise his own faith, his own belief in godly principles and his own love for Christ, so he can control himself.

Discuss con-troversial issues. You can foster this internalization through discussion. Adolescents love to talk about life's issues; and the more controversial the issue, the more they love to discuss it. They are trying to gain mastery over their world, and the first step they take in this process is intellectual mastery. They have lengthy "bull sessions" in which they exercise their recently-developed ability to reason abstractly. They go over and over topics without coming to any conclusions. But this is not to say that these discussions are without purpose. On the contrary, they serve several important functions.

First, discussion gives adolescents a chance to relate to their peers. Since the peer group reaches the height of its influence during adolescence, it is very important for an adolescent to learn the give and take of social relationships; he is highly motivated to learn social rules and customs that will gain him acceptance among fellow adolescents. Lengthy discussions can be a training ground for learning such rules and customs as well as providing the rewards of social interaction and semi-productive activity.

Second, and perhaps equally important, discussion sessions on controversial topics enable the adolescent to release sexual and aggressive energy in a socially acceptable manner. Christian principles prohibit unmarried persons from engaging in sexual intercourse and all persons from displaying unbridled aggression. Therefore, young people who choose to follow Christ have a special challenge to learn ways of handling these God-given drives appropriately. Since God won't take away these drives, young people need to channel sexuality and aggression into other activities.

Some of teenagers' most popular "hot" topics are abortion, mercy killing, capital punishment, and premarital sex. By talking about sexuality and aggressive acts, young people release some of the sexual and aggressive energy that builds up within them and, at the same time, slowly settle in their minds (internalize) their own views on these topics.

In family worship, Christian parents should place a heavier emphasis on discussion (with a corresponding decrease in didactic lessons) when their child reaches early adolescence. They should let the young person experience the rewards of open and frank discussion while still under the guidance of his parents. Parents can learn much about where their adolescent stands on a given issue by listening carefully to what he has to say about it.

And engaging in open discussions with his parents will allow an adolescent the independence he needs to express his own opinion and even disagree with his parents on occasion. This method will be much more fruitful with young people than will a lesson taught by parents.

Of course, you will always want to keep your discussions Bible-centered. Read a passage of Scripture—a parable or verses from an epistle—and then discuss at length how this particular passage applies to each person's life. Be specific and try to produce some creative insights. Lorraine Peterson's *If God Loves Me, Why Can't I Get My Locker Open?* * and *Falling Off Cloud Nine**, and William L. Coleman's *The Great Date Wait** provide excellent insights into teenagers' concerns.

Family worship provides an excellent opportunity to translate lofty scriptural principles into everyday, concrete terms. Perhaps you are discussing the eighth commandment, "Thou shalt not steal." This *appears* easy to obey, but is it? What does it mean in day-to-day living? Maybe Dad has been tempted when filing his income tax to disregard a little extra cash he has made "on the side." Maybe Mom received too much change at the supermarket and failed to notify the cashier? What about the "great deal" Brother got on the minibike? Was it fair for him to pay a fraction of its real worth just because the previous owner was in a bind and had to sell at any price?

If these matters are discussed candidly, family members will begin to see the real meaning of Christian discipleship. They will be less tempted to obey the letter of the law rather than the spirit. They will internalize Christian principles.

Let everyone research answers for a topic.

The reverse of this technique is also helpful in keeping discussions Bible-based. Announce a topic of discussion—for example, God's standard for dress—and then let each person find relevant passages of Scripture. Such a topic could be discussed for several days if your family found it interesting. One day could be devoted to specific statements on dress ("... women adorn themselves in

---

*Bethany House Publishers.

modest apparel, with shamefacedness and sobriety; not with braided hair, or gold, or pearls, or costly array," 1 Tim. 2:9). Another day could be set aside for illustrations in the Bible where clothing affected a person's entire life (e.g., Joseph's coat, Achan's stoning because he took a "goodly Babylonish garment"). Eventually you should discuss how God wants a Christian to dress *today*. Here especially you would need to seek God's guidance in your family worship because it is so easy to interpret the Bible according to preconceived ideas. God's call for "modesty" might mean one thing to Mom and Dad and something entirely different to the teenager in the household.

Besides discussions (and lots of them), teenagers need Christ-centered activity in order to retain their enthusiasm for Christianity. Again, this is a means of channeling their abundant sexual and aggressive energy. Young people that aren't involved in some kind of work for the Lord, whether it be witnessing to their peers, teaching younger children, or painting the church, often lose interest in Christianity and may even drop out of the church altogether. Keep your teenager involved—make him feel needed.

There seems to be a parallel between the spiritual growth of a child and the religious development of the church in this generation. When a child is young, he needs to learn of God's abundant love and mercy. He needs to know, above all, that God is his Friend, and that He will withhold no good gift from him. During his middle years, a child learns that God has rules for us to live by, standards that He expects us to uphold. The child learns self-control and self-restraint. Then during adolescence, the young person, with a strong background in God's love and law, begins to focus on activity for the good of others. With the idealism characteristic of youth, he sets out to make the world a better place to live, he seeks to help the downtrodden, and he longs for the church as a whole to get "on fire" for the Lord. All three of these stages are necessary; a person cannot experience sustained Christian growth if he skips one of these steps.

Do you remember the "Jesus people" of the early 1970s? These young people went everywhere telling everyone they met about Jesus. They descended on towns with their pamphlets and their enthusiasm, preached on street corners and in general created much excitement and interest in Jesus.

Their zeal and sincerity was without question, yet we don't hear a thing about them today. This is because they lacked a solid foundation in the Scriptures. They were on fire for God but did not understand the depth of His love or the majesty of His law. Most were eventually absorbed by the established churches which had such a foundation, or they dropped out of Christianity altogether.

Church growth and maturity can be assessed along these same lines. A few years ago some churches promoted the message, "God is love. He loves you and wants you to love Him. Do whatever you want to do as long as it is loving." This philosophy was called situation ethics. There were no absolute rights or wrongs. Everything was judged according to how "loving" an act it was. These churches flourished for a while, but then their memberships began to fall dramatically.

In what appeared to be a wholesale turning away from Christianity, one group of churches flourished—those which believed completely in the Bible as the inspired Word of God and which enjoined their members to obey the explicit commands of God. There were no situation ethics here; rather than have each person decide what was right or wrong on the basis of love, they relied on "Thus saith the Lord." These churches had grasped the message of God's love and had balanced it with the message of His holy requirements. They had progressed along the ladder of Christian growth and had flourished.

But these churches continue to prosper today because they have not neglected the third stage of Christian growth—*outreach*. This stage corresponds to the adolescent's need for Christian work and witnessing, and is just as vital to the church as it is to the adolescent. Without a reaching beyond self, without a self-sacrificing interest in others, Christianity eventually weakens and dies. Love, obedience, and self-sacrifice must be the cornerstones of Christ's work on earth. All these ingredients are essential, both for the church and for the individual. Consider your adolescent's interests and gifts, but by all means encourage him, both through precept and example, to work for God.

116

**Study
doctrinal
beliefs.**

Since adolescence is a time of doubt and re-
bellion, you may confront these problems in your
young person. If he is open to doing some serious
study, you can use family worship to clear up his
doubts and questions. For instance, your teen-
ager might question why he has to go to church. This would be an
ideal time to conduct a series of studies on the history of the
Church: how it began (Acts 2), how it developed (remainder of
Acts), God's purpose for the Church (Eph. 5:27), where it stands
today (Rev. 2 and 3), where the Church is going (Rev. 7 through
20), and the Church's final reward (Rev. 21 and 22). If certain
doctrines of the church present problems to your adolescent,
spend some time going over the scriptural texts which form the
basis of your beliefs.

Anna Mow has pinpointed several other areas of concern to
adolescents. Perhaps you will want to cover some of these during
home worship:

> Many youths raised in Christian homes have problems of
> guilt and unforgiveness which they cannot handle. They want to
> know how to get along with their parents. They want to know
> how to be a Christian on a date. They worry about the Trinity
> and other theological questions. They wonder how to know the
> will of God, how to pray, how to understand the Bible. They are
> often worried about science and their faith. Many ask, "Is it God
> talking to me or is it just my desires?" In their hearts they
> wonder about all the things that have bothered man from the
> beginning. They are often more serious than their elders. And
> they are more serious at a younger age than we think.*

Don't forget the basic issues which the adolescent must face:
total commitment to God, choice of vocation, and choice of a life
partner. Adolescence is a time of rapid growth and change. With
God's help and a strong family to back him up, your adolescent

*Your Child from Birth to Rebirth, p. 44.

can emerge from this turbulent time with a strong faith and emotional maturity to face the many questions and challenges of adult life.

18. Adults

It is difficult to describe any typical worship format that will benefit all adults. Personal interests, vocational background, time availability, etc., vary so much from person to person that what works for one person or family may not suit another. The basic format of prayer, Bible study, and singing can be modified almost infinitely to satisfy all ages and life-styles.

Adult worship can take three basic forms: private devotions, parents praying together for their children, and the family altar. Each has its unique place in an adult's Christian growth and each serves an essential purpose in the Christian life.

In private devotions, an individual comes alone before God and communes with Him. Private devotions formed the core of Jesus' life—"He went out into a mountain to pray, and continued all night in prayer to God" (Luke 6:12). This is a time to become intimately acquainted with God, to tell Him our troubles, to gain solutions to problems, to receive comfort for cares, and to procure strength to meet trials. Even more important, private devotions gives God access to our lives; it enables Him to "take the stony heart out of [our] flesh, and . . . give [us] an heart of flesh" (Ezek. 11:19). Without *personal* fellowship with God, without a personal dedication of ourselves to Him, our corporate worship can become empty and meaningless.

A second form of adult worship focuses mainly on parents' concern for their children's welfare. This type of worship has been called "family covenant praying"; it involves presenting our children to God—their strengths, their weaknesses, their joys, their disappointments—and asking His blessing and protection for them. Christian parents are recognizing that God in times past saved *families*: Noah and his family were protected from the deluge; Lot and his family were delivered from Sodom; the jailer of Phillipi believed "in God with all his house"; Lydia was "baptized and her household." Parents are claiming the promise of Isaiah 49:25: "For I will contend with him that contendeth with thee, and I will save thy children."

Parents can act as priests of their households, presenting their children to God, invoking His blessing on them, and securing the Holy Spirit's presence with them. Then, acting as prophets, they can present God to their children, telling them of His mercy and love.

One woman I know has a new and deepened relationship with God because her mother regularly prayed for her and the rest of the household. Although the mother had been divorced for many years and thus was unable to pray with her husband, she and another woman agreed to meet once a week for the express purpose of praying for their children. They kept their weekly appointment for many months with no apparent results. The mother had mentioned to my friend very casually, "Sue and I meet together once a week to pray for our children." This thought—that her mother cared enough about her salvation to pray for her—struck a responsive chord in the woman. The Holy Spirit was working in her, preparing her to meet Jesus as her Savior, and revealing her great need for Christ. Eventually she experienced true conversion for the first time in her life, even though she grew up "in the church." She now meets weekly with other Christian women who pray for their husbands, children, and parents. Love and family covenant praying have come full circle.

The third form of adult worship centers around the family altar. This, of course, will vary, depending upon the makeup of the family. If there are children at home, worship will, for the most part, be geared to their needs and levels of maturity. Since age-related types of worship have been covered earlier, let's now discuss various worship formats suitable for adults.

Read through the Bible. Christian adults, hopefully, have reached intellectual maturity and spiritual stability. They are ready for intensive Bible study. Many families have chosen to read the Bible from Genesis through Revelation, a goal which can be reached in about one year (three chapters a day are read for six days and four chapters are read on the seventh day). Each family member brings his own Bible and takes a turn reading a specified number of verses. Several different versions of the Bible might also be used to add interest and understanding.

One evening my husband and I joined two other families for family worship. We sang familiar hymns accompanied by both a piano and an organ (a glorious luxury). Each person was then given a Bible from which to read. Every person in the group, except our host, was given the King James Version. Our host, however, had the New International Version. Before we began to read the designated chapters, our host set the scene of the narrative—David's flight from Naioth. Each of us took turns reading several verses while the rest followed the text in their Bibles. I, unfortunately, found it difficult to follow the story as I desired—to see it as an actual event in the life of a real man—to relive it. But when our host read from the new version, the up-to-date vocabulary and sentence structure made the narrative come alive for me. Suddenly I could identify with David and his plight.

Read one chapter of Proverbs every day. Rather than reading the Bible from beginning to end, some families prefer to study certain portions of the Bible in depth. Several people I know receive rich blessings from reading one chapter of Proverbs each day for a month. Since there are thirty-one chapters, they read the chapter which corresponds to the date (e.g., on the eighth, they read Proverbs 8). When a new month begins, "recycle" and again read Proverbs 1. One pastor and his wife even read their daily chapter of Proverbs twice: once quickly in the morning as they begin their day and once slowly and thoughtfully, with plenty of discussion time, in the evening.

The Psalms lend themselves to in-depth study. One family in

which both father and son-in-law are pastors regularly recites entire psalms together from memory. If they stumble in their recitation, they make that psalm the subject of specific study and memorization.

Recite psalms from memory.

For variety you might want to try a self-evaluation on a certain subject. If the subject is relationships, follow this procedure:

Conduct a Christian self-evaluation

(1) Let each adult list the characteristics of Christian human relationships—those things that he especially considers uniquely Christlike. Try to be concrete; rather than saying, "A Christian is kind to others," state the idea in more specific terms—"A Christian goes out of his way to help someone in need—someone who is ill, grieving, etc."

(2) Have each person list his own strengths in dealing with others.

(3) Have each person list his weaknesses.

(4) Have each person tell what he has discovered about himself.

(5) Have the members of the worship group pray for each other.

(6) Read Romans 12 aloud during worship time for a week. (This chapter deals specifically with interpersonal relationships.)

Adapt this procedure for self-evaluations in areas such as prayer, anxiety, temptation, finance, honesty, self-image, commitment, discipline, and self-control.

Many excellent devotional books also are available for family or personal worship. Several classics and contemporary devotional books are listed in the Appendix.

Prayer is, of course, a vital part of adult worship. Through prayer we develop intimacy with God and receive strength and wisdom to live victoriously. In *A Man Called Peter*, Catherine Marshall relates how she and her husband often spent a short time together in prayer, first thing in the morning. They refrained from this practice only when it became routine or superfi-

122

cial. Mrs. Marshall testifies that on those mornings when they prayed, things went smoothly and all family members got along well. But on those mornings when they failed to pray, it seemed that innumerable little things went wrong. The few minutes spent each morning—just the two of them, aside from their regular family worship—proved themselves powerful.

19. Different Ages

Each of the previous chapters in this section dealt with one age group and presented worship formats tailored to that age group. However, few families consist of just one or two children in a single age group. Most families have children of various ages, interests, and needs. How can parents make worship meaningful for everyone?

Of course, no single answer can fit the great variety of family circumstances. But consider how other families have solved this dilemma. One family with two-year-old twin boys and a five-year-old girl has set up a system of progressive family worship. They begin just before the boys' bedtime; the entire family gathers, sings a special song with actions for the boys, prays a short prayer, and sings a prayer song. Then it's off to bed with the twins!

A few minutes later Mother or Dad has a special worship hour just for their daughter. Parent and child read a Bible story (or stories teaching biblical principles), sing, say the Ten Commandments together, recite a poem, study a Bible lesson and pray. They also talk about the day's activities, both good and bad; this gives the parent an excellent opportunity to point his daughter to Jesus for comfort, assurance, strength, and courage.

After Daughter goes to bed, then Mom and Dad each take time for private devotions. Finally, Mom and Dad conclude their evening worship by meeting together for Bible study and prayer. This is a time to discuss insights received in their private devotions, a time to gain strength from one another.

Some parents of preschoolers and older children have found it helpful to begin with a *short* period of worship for the whole family (perhaps a prayer, a song and a brief Bible study geared to the preschooler's interest), followed by a time of deeper Bible study and discussion for the older members of the family. During this second half of worship, the preschooler draws or colors a picture depicting the Bible passage the others are reading and discussing. This gives him something to do with his hands (far better than a nagging, "Sit still and be quiet") and also encourages him to pay attention to the Bible passage under study. He listens carefully for different details of the narrative to include in his picture.

Different versions for different age levels. If the family consists of children with different levels of reading ability, members could read aloud the same verses of Scripture, each from a different Bible translation. Younger children could use the paraphrased versions or children's Bible stories while older children and parents could read more traditional versions. After each person reads his translation, he gives his own interpretation of what the verses mean. The family then discusses the basic concepts of the verses, as well as the different shades of meaning they have discovered from the various translations.

PART FOUR

Twenty-four Hours a Day

20. Home Worship as a Way of Life

"O how love I thy law! it is my meditation all the day" (Ps. 119:97).

Formal home worship, as important as it is, can never replace the "fleshing out" of biblical Christianity in every moment of our daily lives. A lesson studied during evening worship will have its full impact only when its message is applied to specific experiences in the lives of family members.

God enjoined the Israelites to practice the attitude of worship constantly. He commanded, ". . . And thou shalt . . . talk of them when thou sittest in thine house, and when thou walkest by the way, and when thou liest down, and when thou risest up" (Deut. 6:7). Our family worship, the instruction of our children, and our personal relationship with God cannot be isolated events, quarantined from the rest of our daily activities. Our worship of God must be so entwined with every aspect of our lives that we cannot possibly separate ourselves from Him without completely restructuring our existence. This may sound vague and idealistic but in practice it is a simple and joyful way of life. It is a matter of sharing all of your life with God.

A seventeenth-century monk, Brother Lawrence, decided that he would experience God's presence all day long, communing with God no matter what he was doing or what was happening to him. However, *The Practice of the Presence of God** (the

*Fleming H. Revell and Baker Book House.

128

title of his book) came no more naturally to him than it does to us. Brother Lawrence had to *work* at it.

He began by spending a lengthy period of time each morning just thinking about the reality of God—His power, His majesty, His great love. He continued this practice until his unconscious mind, as well as his rational intellect, believed the truth of God's existence.

Lawrence's next step was to spend every spare minute in prayer. In this manner, he developed the habit of sharing his whole life with God.

Finally he began talking with God no matter what he was doing—cooking (his responsibility in the monastery), walking, bathing, etc. Eventually it became as natural for him to feel God's presence as it had been before to miss it. The promise, "Draw nigh to God, and he will draw nigh to you" (James 4:8), became a reality for Brother Lawrence. It can be a reality for us as well.

Children, too, can learn to sense God's presence in every aspect of their lives. New parents spend endless hours rocking, feeding, and comforting their infant. These times are excellent opportunities to fill a tiny child's mind with songs about Jesus and His love.

Once children learn to talk, our opportunities and responsibilities broaden. Many Christian educators believe that God gives children an innate capacity to respond to His love. We parents have innumerable chances to foster this sensitivity to God in our children if we will only take the time and trouble to do so. We can talk with our children about Jesus as we go about our daily activities with them, as we take walks together, as they help us with household tasks, as we eat meals together.

Teach "on-the-spot" lessons. We can imitate Christ's method of using the familiar situations of life to teach spiritual lessons. As we search for a missing shoe, we can tell our child the parable of the lost coin. As we garden together, we can tell the parable of the sower or tell how our self-life must be buried (like the seeds) before a Christlike life can emerge (like the beautiful plants). These "on-the-spot" lessons will make deep impressions on young minds as well as teach our children to look for Christ's love in every part of life. They will help our children understand that worship is far more than felt boards or Bible picture books.

Frequently children who already know Jesus will talk about Him spontaneously throughout the day. Their favorite words of consolation might be, "Don't worry, Jesus will make you feel better." They offer this bit of sympathy and encouragement to other children, to adults, and even to animals. This not only provides a witness to those around them, it also gives Mom and Dad many chances to talk with the child about Jesus' love and care for everyone. One child I know is fascinated with the thought of flying when she gets to heaven. If she sees a mountain or the moon, she immediately thinks, "Jesus will teach me how to fly up there"—nothing will be too high or too distant to reach. Her mother usually exploits this thought and discusses with the child how wonderful heaven will be.

One advantage of this method of worship is that the child is already interested in discussing Jesus; *he* introduces the subject rather than having it forced upon him. After all, very few people—adults or children—like to have their activities interrupted to listen to a formal religious discourse. How much better if we weave the lesson into normal conversation, making it an integral part of the child's world rather than some isolated unit.

Questions which our children inevitably ask offer us another opportunity to point them toward Christ. Answer all children's questions as best you can, not only to satisfy their curiosity but, more important, to keep the lines of communication open. This can be a big assignment, especially during the years when every other word is "Why?" But willingness to talk about any topic when the child is two can develop trust and communication that will carry parent and child through the difficult years of adolescence. Too many parents ignore the unceasing questions of their toddlers only to lament the absence of meaningful communication with their troubled adolescents. They long for their teenagers to come to them with their doubts, questions, and aspirations; but often the teenagers won't come because they were turned away as small children.

A thoughtful parent can use a child's questions in three ways. First, a parent can pass on knowledge, values, and wisdom as he answers the multitude of questions a child asks. He can teach the child of God's great love, His creative power, His watchcare over us, and His holiness. If the toddler fears thunder storms and asks, "Daddy, what's happening?", Father can explain calmly and simply that God is in control and will take care of His children in any situation. If a preteenager asks, "Why did Ginger's older sister get married and quit school in the middle of the year?", Mom has an excellent opportunity to discuss the value of obeying God's laws concerning sexual abstinence before marriage. Such day-to-day bits of information, rather than long formal lectures or sermons, can give a child the best preparation for a life with Christ. Gradually, all that he hears will begin to fit together like a puzzle as he pieces it together himself.

Second, parents can use a child's question to promote a close parent-child relationship. As he receives honest, straightforward answers from an interested parent, a child learns to rely on the parent when he needs help, information or just encouragement. He learns to trust his parent, who, in turn, can teach him to trust and love God.

Third, a parent can learn a lot about a child, an adolescent, or another adult by listening carefully to what he has to say. This applies, of course, to general conversation as well as questions. If eight-year-old Johnny asks, "What is a joint?", his parents had better discover where he heard this word and who Johnny is associating with at school, as well as explaining what they know about drugs.

Sometimes the tables are turned, and children can teach adults the importance of making God a vital part of life. One group of school children was excitedly putting up Christmas decorations when a dispute broke out among them about the arrangement of the ornaments. They argued heatedly for several minutes. Finally they decided that their harsh feelings were destroying the spirit of Christmas. They took all the ornaments down and agreed not to put them back up until they once again felt love in their hearts for each other. Two days passed and still no ornaments brightened the room. Finally, on the third day, the spirit of dissension in the classroom changed to one of peace, love, and forgiveness. The children put up the decorations, praising God for His working in their lives.

21. Informal Worship Through Music and Prayer

Use Christian music records or tapes.

Music can play an important part in the life of a child, so why not use this medium to lead your child to Christ? An inexpensive phonograph or tape player and a few well-chosen Christian records or tapes for children can give a youngster hours of enjoyment and inspiration. You don't need many records—two or three long-playing ones will give a child plenty of variety. In fact, children love repetition; by hearing the same songs over and over, they memorize the words and eventually sing along with the record. Well-learned songs become old friends; soon your child will be singing and humming them all day long.

Here are several recordings and artists which your child will enjoy: "The Music Machine" and the other Agapeland albums (Birdwing/Sparrow) teach biblical principles in a delightful manner; the Bill Gaither Trio has produced several albums that appeal to children, as has Evie Tornquist Karlsson; Gary and Carol Johnson's albums, "Come," "Thanks," and "Reminded of His Goodness" (Bethany House Publishers), provide unique treatments of Scripture passages; Maranatha's "Praise" I-V, as well as "Kid's Praise Album," vols. 1 & 2 (Maranatha/Word), are very popular recordings.

Play music at special times.

Use your imagination as you think of opportunities for your child to hear his recordings. Play them while you fold clothes together—this has been almost a ritual at our house. Play them while your child is coloring or painting, or while he cleans up his room. As a special treat, let your child listen to one record before his nap or bedtime. Many times he will become so relaxed he will fall asleep before the record ends. And most special of all, hold your child in your lap and rock him while you both listen to the songs or sing along together.

Certainly you will want to sing to your child throughout the day. And don't worry about your singing ability—this won't matter one bit to your child! Sing while you're cooking, dusting, or going for a walk. Sing both hymns and children's songs. The atmosphere of love for Christ will fill your home and your child's memories.

Prayer

Informal prayer outside of the worship period can be a powerful tool for training children. One minister I know has suggested that since we as adults must "wrestle not against flesh and blood, but against principalities, against powers, against the rulers of the darkness of this world, against spiritual wickedness in high places" (Eph. 6:12), the same must be true for our children. And children, because of their innocence and naïveté, seem especially susceptible to the darts of Satan, as well as to the whispers of the Holy Spirit. The minister advised parents to pray with their children when they were having a "bad day" rather than scolding them. Thus, the child's consciousness would be turned to God.

Pray when your child has a bad day. This is highly practical, spiritual advice. When your child won't obey, refuses to share, or is hopelessly fussy, pray with him, asking the Holy Spirit to fill the child's heart, and command Satan to depart. Assure your child that Christ will help him live a godly life. Of course, this would be a good way to begin every day.

Prayer before putting children to bed is a good practice, too. Ideally both parents should pray with the children before bedtime. One father had the practice of spending about twenty minutes with each child before bed. They would discuss the day's events, go over anything troubling the child (or parents), and talk about special joys of the day. Then the father would put the child in bed and tell him something like this, "I love you very much and will always love you, no matter what you do. If you ever need a friend, you can always count on me." This took quite a bit of time every night—about two hours—for the man had six children. But it paid off. Today those six children love the Lord and have devoted their lives to His service.

Let your child pray for you. Sometimes parents need their children's prayers, too. One mother related how she went to her children and apologized for handling a situation poorly. She explained that parents make mistakes, too, and that we all need Jesus' help every minute of the day, even after we're adults.

The little girl thought about this a moment, then asked, "Mommy, do you want me to pray for you and Daddy?"

"Oh, yes, I wish you would," her mother replied.

Prayer for each other is part of the cement that holds families together. It is most effective when carried out informally on a daily basis.

It costs much to bring your family before the Lord day after day, week after week—much in prayer, in preparation, in patience (when your efforts seem fruitless), and in persistence (when you are tempted to "let it slide just this once"). It is hard, but it pays eternal dividends. The benefits of home worship come with a price worth paying.

Appendix

Suggested Devotional Aids (categorized by age groups)

Six months to two years
1. Use real objects as much as possible.
2. For information on felts, check your local Christian bookstore, or write: Child Evangelism Center, Box 19009, 320 W. St. Joseph St., Lansing, MI 48901 (telephone: 517-485-2226, ext. 61).

Two through three years
1. Arch Books (Concordia Publishing House, St. Louis, MO). Over eighty different Bible stories by various authors. Children love to listen to the accompanying records or tapes.
2. *The Bible in Pictures for Little Eyes* by Kenneth N. Taylor (Moody Press, Chicago, IL). Nearly 200 very short Bible stories with accompanying illustrations.
3. *My Bible Friends* by Etta B. Degering (Review and Herald Publishing Assoc., Washington, D.C.). Ten volumes of beautifully illustrated, simple Bible stories. Can be used until a child reaches four or five.
4. *Today I Feel Like a Warm Fuzzy* by William L. Coleman (Bethany House Publishers, Minneapolis, MN). Helpful discussions of children's emotions. Helps children understand and accept their feelings.
5. *Today I Feel Loved!* by William L. Coleman. Sequel to above book.
6. One-Year Bible Story in Felt. All the felts you will need to teach almost any story from the Bible. Write Child Evangelism Center at the address given above.

Four through five years
1. *Bible Stories for Family Devotions* by Jo Ann Merrell (Bethany

House Publishers, Minneapolis, MN). Formerly titled *Tree of Life.* An excellent book for generating interest and excitement in the Bible. Each story has a leaf sticker which is attached to a poster-sized tree.

2. *Counting Stars* by William L. Coleman (Bethany House Publishers, Minneapolis, MN). Fifty-two devotionals filled with facts about God's creation, with scriptures and thought questions.

3. *The Golden Book of Bible Stamps* by Jane Werner (Golden Press, Racine, WI). Forty-eight short Bible stories with a black-and-white picture to color and a brightly colored stamp to place on each page.

4. *The Good Night Book* by William L. Coleman (Bethany House Publishers. Minneapolis, MN). Fifty-two devotionals especially written for little ones who may be afraid of the dark. Many fascinating illustrations from nature.

5. *Singing Penguins and Puffed-Up Toads* by William L. Coleman (Bethany House Publishers, Minneapolis, MN). Devotionals about sea creatures, each with a concluding moral and an appropriate scripture.

6. Gospel-Graphs (Scripture Press Publications, Wheaton, IL). Paper figures to use on flannel boards to teach lessons on obedience, love, etc.

Six through nine years

1. *The Child's Story Bible* by Catherine F. Vos, edited by Marianne Ralins (Wm. B. Eerdmans, Grand Rapids, MI). Well-told stories, but unfortunately, not many illustrations.

2. *Egermeier's Bible Story Book* by Elsie E. Egermeier (Warner Press, Anderson, IN). Old and New Testament stories in biblical order. Good illustrations.

3. *Forty-five Simple Object Talks for Children* by Barbara Ebert and Ruth S. Odor (Standard Publishing Co., Cincinnati, OH). Bible lessons using objects from a child's everyday world.

4. *Listen to the Animals* by William L. Coleman (Bethany House Publishers. Minneapolis, MN). Each devotional has a story about an animal. An appropriate Bible passage, and questions to stimulate the child's thinking.

5. *My Magnificent Machine* by William L. Coleman (Bethany House Publishers, Minneapolis, MN). Fascinating glimpses into the workings of various parts of the body.

6. *More About My Magnificent Machine* by William L. Coleman. Sequel to above book.

Ten through thirteen years

1. *A Daily Look at Jesus* by Mary Lillian Miles (Moody Press, Chicago,

IL). Short, relevant devotional thoughts with accompanying scripture to look up, plus a prayer thought.

2. *Does Anyone Care How I Feel?* by Mildred Tengbom (Bethany House Publishers, Minneapolis, MN). Fifty-two devotions to be read by preteens to the rest of the family. Facilitates communication about everybody's real feelings.

3. *Joshua Wiggins and the King's Kids* by Charles Beamer (Bethany House Publishers, Minneapolis, MN). Fifty devotional segments divided into ten continuing adventure stories. Keeps the youngsters eager for the next installment.

4. *Lord, I Have a Question* by Betty Westrom Skold (Augsburg Publishing House, Minneapolis, MN). Devotional stories for preteen girls.

5. *On Your Mark* by William L. Coleman (Bethany House Publishers, Minneapolis, MN). Stories of well-known athletes demonstrate biblical virtues. Bible passages, thought questions and photographs.

The teenage years

1. *Day by Day* by Amy Bolding (Baker Book House, Grand Rapids, MI). Scripture and a brief devotional thought for each day of the year. Also try *Dynamic Fingertip Devotions* by the same author.

2. *If God Loves Me, Why Can't I Get My Locker Open?* by Lorraine Peterson (Bethany House Publishers, Minneapolis, MN). Ninety-one short devotionals with scripture passages, questions. Discusses relevant teenage issues. Humorous cartoon illustrations.

3. *Falling Off Cloud Nine and Other High Places* and *Why Isn't God Giving Cash Prizes?* by Lorraine Peterson. Sequels to above book.

4. *I'm Not Mad at God* by David Wilkerson (Bethany House Publishers. Minneapolis. MN). A candid look at the struggles and victories of a man who has worked extensively with young adults.

5. *Just Between God and Me* by Sandra Drescher (Zondervan Publishing House, Grand Rapids, MI). Devotional thoughts for every day of the year. Includes scripture passages and prayer thoughts for early teens.

6. *Remember Now* by Walter D. Cavert (Abingdon Press, Nashville, TN). Scripture passages to look up and a relevant devotional thought.

7. *Winning Words* by Curtis French (Word Books, Waco, TX). Devotions designed especially for athletes.

Adults

1. *Climbing the Heights* by Al Bryant (Zondervan Publishing House, Grand Rapids, MI). Devotionals for the entire year taken from

writings of great people of God.

2. *A Day at a Time* by Richard Halverson (Zondervan Publishing House, Grand Gapids, MI). Daily devotional readings for men.

3. *Day by Day* by Andrew Murray (Bethany House Publishers, Minneapolis, MN). Readings for every day of the year by the famous nineteenth-century devotional writer.

4. *Love Songs* by Al Bryant (Word Books, Waco, TX). Daily meditations for married couples designed to keep the intimate relationship of marriage fresh and alive.

6. *Our Daily Bread* by M. R. DeHaan and Henry G. Bosch (Zondervan Publishing House, Grand Rapids, MI). Devotionals for each day of the year. Very interesting and relevant.

7. *Salt in My Kitchen* by Jeanette Lockerbie (Moody Press, Chicago, IL). Devotionals for women. Very interesting anecdotes to accompany scripture passages.

8. *More Salt in My Kitchen* by Jeanette Lockerbie. Sequel to above.

9. *My Utmost for His Highest* by Oswald Chambers (Dodd, Mead & Co., New York, NY). A devotional classic for each day of the year.

For all ages

1. *The Amen Game* by Brush Bradley (Bethany House Publishers, Minneapolis, MN). A Bingo-type game which requires no Bible knowledge to win, but teaches many Bible facts as the game is played.

2. *Celebrate the Feasts* by Martha Zimmerman (Bethany House Publishers, Minneapolis, MN). Make the Old Testament come alive by observing the Hebrew feasts with your family.

3. *Devotions for Your Family* by Marjorie Bloom (Word Books, Waco, TX). An excellent study of the book of Mark with suggestions for use with any age from four and up.

4. *Games*, compiled by Mary Hohenstein (Bethany House Publishers). Contains many games for all ages that make learning about the Bible enjoyable (includes other types of games as well).

5. *Your Family Worship Guidebook* by Reuben Herring (Broadman Press, Nashville, TN). Specific devotional ideas for discussion. A scripture passage is given and then several questions follow which make the passage relevant to everyday life. Questions are designed for varying age groups. Helps the whole family to be involved.

Bibliography

Christenson, Evelyn. *What Happens When Women Pray*. Wheaton, Illinois: Victor Books, 1978.

Christenson, Larry. *The Christian Family*. Minneapolis, Minnesota: Bethany Fellowship, Inc., 1970.

Ebert, Barbara, and Odor, Ruth Shannon. *45 Simple Object Talks for Children*. Cincinnati, Ohio: Standard Publishing, 1970.

Martin, Dorothy. *Creative Family Worship*. Chicago, Illinois: Moody Press, 1977.

Mow, Anna B. *Your Child from Birth to Rebirth*. Grand Rapids, Michigan: Zondervan Publishing House, 1976.